MW00778174

Doña Tules

Doña Tules

Santa Fe's Courtesan and Gambler

Mary J. Straw Cook

UNIVERSITY OF NEW MEXICO PRESS ～ ALBUQUERQUE

© 2007 by the University of New Mexico Press
All rights reserved. Published 2007
Printed in the United States of America
13 12 11 10 09 08 07   1 2 3 4 5 6 7

Library of Congress Cataloging-in-Publication Data

Cook, Mary J. Straw (Mary Jean Straw)
Doña Tules : Santa Fe's courtesan and gambler / Mary J. Straw Cook.
p. cm.
Includes bibliographical references and index.
ISBN 978-0-8263-4313-0 (cloth : alk. paper)
1. Barceló, Gertrudis, d. 1852. 2. Santa Fe (N.M.)—Biography.
3. Prostitutes—New Mexico—Santa Fe—Biography. 4. Women gamblers—New
Mexico—Santa Fe—Biography. 5. Gamblers—New Mexico—Santa Fe—Biography.
6. Businesswomen—New Mexico—Santa Fe—Biography. 7. Frontier and pioneer
life—New Mexico—Santa Fe. 8. Santa Fe (N.M.)—History—19th century.
9. Santa Fe (N.M.)—Social life and customs—19th century.
10. New Mexico—History—19th century. I. Title.
F804.S253B373 2007
978.9'5603092—dc22
[B]
2007015450

Design and Composition: Melissa Tandysh

For Edward

Contents

Preface

It was a flat, drought-ridden terrain littered with the bleached bones of animals amid abandoned U.S. military equipment from the U.S.–Mexican War of 1846. Among the animal carcasses, human bones hastily buried beside the route were unceremoniously laid bare only to be reclaimed by the *llano* sands, a mercurial burial ground for those who dared to cross it.

The old *jornada* loomed before the Frenchman, his companion-guide, and perhaps several others, their chins buried against their chests to brace against the wind and stinging cold. Centuries before, other travelers had struggled with their swaying, overloaded *carretas*, the solid wooden wheels squealing and groaning with every turn. The grinding sounds announced their presence to lurking Indians awaiting a deadly raid. Each carreta was filled to overflowing with precious belongings that signaled the wayfarers' hope of finding a new life in northern Nueva España, New Spain. Instead, the optimistic travelers discovered relentless starvation and misery.

In January 1852 the travelers hurried northward toward Santa Fe along the fifty-mile Jornada del Muerto, Journey of the Dead Man. One rider wrapped a tightly woven serape closer to his body to stem the unbroken jornada wind. His animal heard the familiar words *agua y hierba, agua y hierba*—water and grass, a futile reminder to a thirsty and hungry animal whose sensitive nostrils detected these essentials far in advance of any human calculation. Ahead lay El Contadero, a *paraje*, or resting place, for man and beasts after a long day's journey. It was nothing more than an unmarked place between the lava flows of the

Contadero Mesa and the *cienagas*, or marshes, of the meandering Río Grande. The paraje, nevertheless, meant mesquite and dried cattle dung for fuel, and thus warm food, perhaps the first in several days. A diet of cold jerky or dried meat was the weary wayfarer's first salvation, his God a close second.

The San Andrés to the east and the San Cristóbal Mountains to the west surrounded the paraje. They appeared familiar, as well they should. This was the Frenchman's third trip across the jornada in less than six months, a monumental feat for any Catholic clergyman in this desolate land, including that of the vicar who had accompanied him to Durango, Mexico. But the bitter January wind of 1852 painfully reminded l'Auvergnat that this was his first winter crossing of the jornada. It was not for the spiritually or physically weak.[1]

Born to *paysans aisés*, well-to-do peasants, the Frenchman from the Department of Auvergne exhibited a priestly fragility, which now ached from the New Mexico cold. Before sailing from Le Havre for America a dozen years earlier the priest commissioned a Parisian tailor on the narrow Rue du Bac on the left bank of the Seine River to make a cloak of heavy black-dyed cloth used by the Auvergnat mountaineers. He also had wisely requested that extra linings of cashmere be added for warmth.[2]

A brief four months earlier, in 1851, the Frenchman had crossed this same waterless shortcut on El Camino Real de Tierra Adentro, the Royal Road to the Interior, linking Mexico City to the northern outpost of New Mexico—Santa Fe, meaning Holy Faith. Now, in 1852, the native of Puy-de-Dôme was returning from a thirty-five-hundred-mile round trip southward to Durango, Mexico, crossing the shifting sand hills near Chihuahua and on to the Río Grande at Paso del Norte (El Paso). A leaden cathedral bell in Chihuahua had called the faithful to Mass from miles around. Had more silver gone into its casting, readily available in nearby hills, the clarion ring might have reached the unfaithful as well.

On his arrival in Durango, which previously included the province of New Mexico, the new French vicar had produced documents to the Mexican bishop José Antonio Laureano López de Zubiría de Escalante. In 1833 the bishop of Durango had actually visited his exuberant flock in Santa Fe and had done so two times more.[3] Each journey to New Mexico had sent a grateful Bishop Zubiría home with his scalp intact, though his vestments were tattered from kisses of adoration. According to one commentator, "The good old man was glad to return with any hem to his garment, so great was the respect paid to him."[4] Had the official decree addressed to him from Rome arrived promptly, a word unknown in the Southwest, he would have read, "The Bishop of Durango be clearly informed . . ." A new bishopric, carved out of his own jurisdiction and larger than France, had been created. The newly appointed vicar apostolic from Santa Fe arrived on Bishop Zubiría's ecclesiastical doorstep to lay claim to his new authority. There was disagreement about the geographical boundaries of the new bishopric.

News from Rome to Mexico had traveled much slower than expected, and the prelate's arrival in Santa Fe in August 1851 had taken both New Mexican priests and parishioners by surprise. An unknown French-speaking priest to replace a Spanish-speaking Mexican in an area earlier a part of Spain and more recently of Mexico? Quite obviously, the Italian pope failed to perceive the importance of appointing a native-born son as bishop, one who understood the manners and mores of the newly acquired area, the bounty of the U.S.–Mexican War.

As the numbing cold stiffened his god-fearing extremities, the Frenchman perhaps pondered his recent combative encounter with a disarmingly gracious, captivating, and well-nourished Bishop Zubiría. His concentration surely included the scanning of the jornada landscape for possible marauding Indians. During this, his third trip, there were no flowered arches or fervent parishioners to welcome him along the route of the Río Grande valley to Santa Fe. Doubtless, the people knew nothing of the Frenchman's return trip through their villages after a mere two months.

Against wind and time, men and pack animals continued to push northward to reach the parish church in Santa Fe known as La Parroquia. The newly appointed vicar apostolic, yet to officially assume his office as titular bishop of Agathonica, had chosen it in favor of La Castrense, a small military chapel on the plaza used by Spanish soldiers and their families since the eighteenth century. The mud walls and interiors of both churches desperately needed repairs. Such obstacles and even more insurmountable difficulties lay before him but in his naïveté and zeal the Frenchman chose to ignore these realities. He felt himself destined to lead New Mexico out of the wilderness and to become the religious leader

of a destitute and uneducated people in an outpost of the American
Catholic Church.

The Frenchman received news by some southbound traveler that an
important and wealthy Santa Fe woman was on the doorstep of death.
He quickly picked up speed, hoping to arrive in time. He left Zubiría's
former vicar forane behind somewhere along the route. But the corpulent red-headed vicar was soon robbed of nineteen mules and four
horses by the Apaches on the Jornada del Muerto, which "left the reverend father nearly afoot."[5]

The Frenchman pressed onward with increased vigor. He gained a
moment's warmth by blowing into his numbed hands, rubbing them
together almost as if in anticipation of God's unfinished work. As he rode
into the wind, he surely contemplated one of the immediate tasks awaiting him in Santa Fe—the burial of Doña María Gertrudis Barceló, the
woman known as Santa Fe's grand dame of monte, fashion, and seduction. Arrangements for her funeral Mass had been hastily consummated
before the new vicar left for the lengthy trip to Durango. He would need
the large sum of money the funeral would provide for future church
projects. Burial details were perhaps handled by the secular Father
José de Jesús Luján, who had previously received a censure by Mexican
bishop Zubiría and would soon be censured by the new prelate.[6]

Born around 1812, Father Luján possessed more than a mere pen-
chant for the fairer sex.[7] After a succession of mistresses or common-law
wives he had sired two children whom he publicly declared legitimate
by a decision of the territorial legislature of February 2, 1878.[8] It was
common knowledge that the priest was living in a most scandalous
manner, keeping a very young and beautiful married woman in his
house. Despite pleas by her husband and orders by the new French prelate to return her to her home, Luján refused to do so, sneeringly calling
the bishop a hypocrite and worse. The Frenchman promptly suspended
him for two years. Sans surplice and visibly consumed with grief, the
crying priest had once followed the coffin of one of his *amantes* through
the unpaved streets of Santa Fe to the old parish church.[9] If indeed Father
Luján was responsible for arranging the solemn ceremony of Gertrudis
Barceló in 1852 it would be well attended by the most prominent government and army figures.[10]

Before leaving Santa Fe for Durango the French cleric had used words in Spanish and English against the drunken chief justice, Grafton Baker, of the New Mexico Supreme Court. Justice Baker declared that he would not surrender his jurisdiction of La Castrense, then being used for the profane purpose of a courtroom and storehouse. And before Baker would do so, he declared publicly that he would hang the bishop and his French friend and vicar general Machebeuf from the same gallows. It was an encounter out of the old West, not between *bandidos* and the law but between the military and high officials of church and state. The matter came to a peaceful resolution in the presence of the ailing Governor James S. Calhoun and other civil authorities.[11]

"They surrendered the building according to all the formalities of the law; the court itself sitting in the church, myself being present, they gave me the keys," wrote the French cleric.[12] The new bishop asserted his ecclesiastical rights for the use of La Castrense. And what better occasion to launch a subscription for money—to repair the crumbling old adobe chapel built almost a century earlier? Contributions came from the governor himself and the repentant chief justice among others, increasing the total amount to one thousand dollars.

Matching funds would be forthcoming, as the French bishop already knew, for burial of the notorious gambler named Gertrudis Barceló in the consecrated ground of La Parroquia would require the new vicar apostolic's permission. And as a result, the empty coffers of the vicar would receive a large cache of specie, money which the French vicar would need to sustain his bishopric until the end of his life in 1888. The choice by Santa Fe's new bishop of the burial in the adobe cathedral of Santa Fe's renowned courtesan and gambler was his decision alone to make. Already showing himself to be a man of decisiveness, he made it and proceeded to leave town amid doubt and rejection by his own clergymen over his right of succession. The lady gambler known as Doña Tules was to receive his benediction during her high funeral Mass. She would pay dearly for her in-church burial. That New Mexico's first bishop buried her at all, and buried her within the Parroquia walls, marked the apotheosis, in death, of her controversial life.

The French graduate of Clermont, born a twin, a chronically ill seminarian who was once called "the Lamb" by his classmates, who had survived two bleedings and fifteen leech treatments on the abdomen, was about to enter the pages of Southwest history in a totally unexpected manner.[13] Simultaneously, a legendary New Mexican woman was about to make her well-choreographed exit from the mortal world. Had these two people met years earlier in Santa Fe, the new vicar apostolic might well have called on her for valuable knowledge, as many powerful, though less pious men had done before him. The French vicar arrived back in Santa Fe on January 10, 1852, six or seven days before the gambler's death, indeed judicious timing for so lengthy a journey.[14] But what should be the subject of his homily at the funeral Mass for this New Mexico courtesan and gambler known as Doña Tules?

Many distinguished Santa Feans would be in attendance in the old parish church, not only out of respect to the deceased, but perhaps out of curiosity to hear the new French vicar, who would alter their lives dramatically over the next three decades. As two earlier eras were ending, the Spanish and the Mexican, another was about to begin—led by the Americans.

CHAPTER ONE

Valle del Río Bavispe, Sonora

～つ

Fruit and young girls ripen early in the sultry Bavispe Valley of east-central Sonora. The narrow but fertile valley parallels the western flank of the Sierra Madre Occidental, separating the Mexican states of Sonora and Chihuahua. Gertrudis Barceló, New Mexico's celebrated gambler and courtesan of the 1830s and 1840s, was born around 1800 in this remote area. She achieved fame by the name of "Tules," said to be the diminutive of Gertrudis, a name that means *fiel a su hogar*, "faithful to her home."[1] She was also known by many other names—"Tula," "Tulas," "Tía Barcelona," "Lona Barcelona," "La Barcelona," "Madam Barcelo," "Señora Toulouse," "Doña Lona," "Doña Julia," "Madam T," and to many, "La Tules."[2]

The origin of the name Tules, suggesting the curvaceousness of her figure, is from the word *tules* meaning "reeds." Tules with a "la" placed before it designates perhaps the one and only, with inference of a slanderous overtone. The nickname may have originated before her arrival in New Mexico in 1815. Coincidentally, tules, or *carrizo agugueado*, grows in the marshes near the villages of Huásabas and Granados in the lower Río Bavispe of Sonora, where the Barcelós live today. It is, therefore, possible that the young and intelligent Gertrudis Barceló first acquired her titillating nickname from the bulrushes surrounding her birthplace.

Whatever the case, Gertrudis Barceló surely discovered early in life her extraordinary perception of and power over the male psyche. Manipulation of men became but one of her many achievements, and to the end of her life she was a genius at the art.[3] Such a talent appears to

FIGURE 1. ❧ "Lady Tules," *Harper's Monthly Magazine*, April 1854.
Museum of New Mexico neg. no. 50815.

FIGURE 2. ❧ Bavispe River near Huásabas, Sonora, Mexico, 1986.
Photo by author.

be the result of astute, native intelligence. It played a significant role in her capacity to read the body language and gambling habits of her often fidgety and sweaty opponents.

Because of apparent chronological discrepancies in Sonoran church records for the late 1700s and early 1800s, Catholic church baptismal records for Gertrudis Barceló or that of her family have not been found.[4] On the 1870 U.S. Census for Valencia County, New Mexico, María de la Luz, younger sister of Gertrudis, gave Sonora as her place of birth. To further help corroborate Sonora as the birthplace of Gertrudis Barceló, her older brother José Trinidad returned to the village of Huásabas following her death in early 1852. In a letter dated 1853 addressed to a Victor Baca in New Mexico, Trinidad Barceló left a significant clue with his return address as Huasavas [*sic*].[5] Barcelós of today remain in the villages of Moctezuma (Oposura), Huásabas, and Granados.[6] They trace their heritage to Antonio Barceló (1717–97), a Spanish marine who participated in the siege of Gibraltar in 1779.[7]

On the northern frontier of New Spain, Huásabas and neighboring

Granados lacked the protection of *presidio* soldiers from Janos or Fronteras. The villages endured incessant raids by nomadic Indian tribes—the Apache, Jano, Jocome, and Suma from the north, and the Seri and occasionally the Pima Alto from the west. These warriors of the *desierto* plundered Sonoran mines, ranches, missions, crops, women, and children. Apache Indians from the upper Gila River basin of southern New Mexico, called Gileños, entered Sonora and escaped with impunity through the Púlpito and Carretas passes to the north. Two centuries of unbridled terror under unstable Spanish rule began in the seventeenth century. The capture of Gerónimo and his tribe in southern New Mexico in 1886 ultimately subdued the wily Apaches.[8]

Between 1790 and 1831 a fragile truce brought peace between the Spanish and the Apaches living in Sonora. The reorganization of defense began in 1765, initiated by the visitor general to New Spain, José de Gálvez, and in 1786 by the *Instrucción* of viceroy Bernardo de Gálvez. Retaliatory expeditions by soldiers against the Indians resulted in a temporary reprieve. Trade alliances with the nomadic tribes plus enticements of food, horses, and liquor encouraged their settlement near the presidios. When the Mexican government stopped the subsistence for lack of funds, Indian dependency ceased and warfare resumed for the remainder of the nineteenth century.[9]

Rugged mountains cut off the narrow north-to-south river valleys such as the Bavispe from all but the Pacific coast. These fertile valleys were the main suppliers of food for colonial Sonora. Today's inhabitants of the lower Río Bavispe, once termed the breadbasket of Sonora, continue to live for the most part in that colonial past, traditionally cultivating two crops annually. Late summer monsoons or tropical storms occasionally cause valley flooding. During the winter months, lighter *equipatas*, or frontal storms, arrive from the Pacific Ocean to the west. Western Sonorans call these subhurricane storms arriving near the feast of St. Francis on October 4, El Cordonazo de San Francisco, the lash of St. Francis.[10]

Indian warfare coupled with the washboard terrain and the geoeconomic isolation of eastern Sonora inevitably shaped the character of its people. Women of La Serrana, the Highland, possessed a fundamental trait from a very early age—survival. Later events in the life of a mature Tules Barceló reveal an intelligent and courageous woman endeavoring to survive in a Spanish, Mexican, and American man's world in any manner possible, including prostitution. To a young and precocious Tules Barceló in remote Sonora, choices in her early life were few—family, home, and anonymity as opposed to wealth and fame. Instinctively and against great odds, she pursued the path that ultimately imprinted her name in the pages of Southwest history.

The Scottish-born, American wife of Spain's first envoy to an independent Mexico in 1839, Fanny Calderón de la Barca, observed how Mexican women occupied their time: "[T]hey do not read, they do not write, they do not go into society. For the most part they do not play, they do not draw . . . nor do they ride on horseback. What they do not do is clear, but what do they do?"[11] What Gertrudis must have concluded was that the *pobres* gambled to amuse themselves. It was a national obsession beginning in childhood.

Interrelated prominent families exercised regional control throughout the state of Sonora, resulting in a distinguished colonial society. Founders of these families, immigrants from northern and eastern Spain, came to Sonora at the end of the colonial period. These immigrants called themselves "notables," dominating the small villages in which they lived. Many made fortunes on the Mexican frontier and owned large estates, but apparently not the Barcelós, or they would have continued living in Sonora.[12]

The date and reason why the Juan Ignacio Barceló family first settled in the Bavispe Valley remains unknown. The Catalán father of Gertrudis, Juan Ignacio, perhaps arrived in Sonora with the Compañía Franca de Voluntarios de Cataluña in 1767. Organized from ranks of the Segundo Regimiento de Infantería Ligera de Cataluña stationed in Barcelona, Spain, the one hundred men and four officers originally destined for Havana, Cuba, were instead sent to New Spain. The Volunteers joined the Sonoran Expedition commanded by Domingo Elizondo. Their mission included not only warfare against the Indians and the expulsion of the Jesuits in 1767 but also the colonization of Sonora. Yet the name of Juan Ignacio Barceló fails to appear on the list of men in the Elizondo Expedition.[13]

Another conjecture to be considered is that perhaps members of the Barceló family migrated earlier from the east, over the Sierra Madre from Chihuahua. The Barceló name survives today in the remote mining

areas of Moris and Chínipas, west of Chihuahua City. During the early
decades of the seventeenth century, Chihuahuan miners crossed over
the Sierras into eastern Sonora seeking silver and gold deposits. Many
remained to farm and raise families. Hindered by heavy seasonal rains
and the flooding of mine shafts, miners soon found mining anything
but a year-round activity. They then focused their daily efforts on farming and stockraising. On his arrival in New Mexico, the older brother of
Tules Barceló, Trinidad, possessed prior knowledge of these professions
plus the advantage of an education.[14]

In 1645 Franciscan father Marcos del Río founded the village of
Huásabas. He named the new mission La Misión de San Francisco Javier
de Guásabas.[15] To the Opatá Indians already living in the Bavispe Valley,
the name of Guásabas in their native tongue meant "where there are many
frogs."[16] On his arrival Fray Marcos found not only indigenous Indians,
but also members of the Mexican-Italian Moreno family. Other names
in the early history of Huásabas include Juan de Mella y Hernández,
born in Galicia, Spain; Don Luis Gonzaga Leyba, a Yaqui Indian; Dons
Guillermo Fimbres and Francisco Xavier Fimbres, Basques from Spain;
and the Durazo family of Italian origin. Once again, the Barceló name
escapes mention before the 1800s in the Bavispe Valley. The Moreno
family history briefly records the marriage of Venancio Durazo Moreno
to a Teresa Barceló Durazo, but with no reference to her parents.[17]

During the 1760s the Barceló name appeared in Arizpe, a presidio
to the northwest of Huásabas. In 1776 Arizpe was the capital of New
Mexico, on the far northern rim of the Viceroyalty of New Spain. Don
Juan Bautista de Anza (1735–88) of Arizpe, Sonora, was New Mexico's
governor. A María Concepción Barceló was the mother of María del
Pilar León who married Josef Joaquín Moraga, *alferez*, or second lieu-
tenant, of Anza's expedition to the coast of California in 1776. It was
on this expedition that Anza founded San Francisco Presidio, Misión
Dolores, Misión Santa Clara, and the pueblo of San José de Guadalupe.
María del Pilar León and Josef Joaquín Moraga are buried at Misión
Dolores in San Francisco.[18]

While the year of arrival of the Barcelós in the Bavispe Valley presently eludes discovery, mission settlements of early Sonora represented
one of greatest successes for the Jesuit order in the New World. The
Jesuits, until their expulsion in 1767, remained the religious guardians

of Sonorans. The village of Huásabas became the mission of one of the better-known Jesuits, Father Juan Nentvig, author of the *Rudo Ensayo*, an essay describing Sonora and Arizona in 1764. Regarding the name of Sonora, Nentvig wrote:

> Although I know nothing of the etymology or origin of the name Sonora, I do not believe I am deceiving myself in being inclined to think it may have been suggested by her great wealth, the news of which swept sonorously across New Spain and into Europe. Perhaps the name might have been given accidentally as has been the case with other provinces of the New World. Still, Sonora, in spite of being assailed by the Apaches, has not failed, nor is she now failing, to conform to the prophecy of the poet who wrote *Conveniunt rebus nomina saepe suis* [names often-times fit their objects]. And as the sound waves of gold and silver spread, so has the fame of Sonora, for there is no portion of this province that does not offer these precious metals, almost on the surface, to those who have the patience to dig and separate the ore from the dirt, or, as it were, the wheat from the chaff.[19]

Until 1815 Juan Ignacio Barceló and his wife, Dolores Herrero, survived Apache attacks to raise a family of three children. The eldest child was José Trinidad, then came María Gertrudis, and the youngest was María de la Luz. We know little about Tules's mother. Juan Ignacio's occupation was undoubtedly that of a farmer or a miner-cattleman, and assuredly that of a gambler. Education of young girls in Sonora was virtually unknown until around 1835.[20] Any education that Tules might have acquired was from her brother Trinidad or through her own immense intellect.[21] On later documents she signed her name followed by a rubric or flourishes when many of her women peers were able only to mark their name with an "x." Unquestionably, to gamble so successfully Tules had to be able to count cards and evaluate the many different sorts of money circulating at the time.[22]

The multicolored soil of Sonora promised metals for the digging, or so Jesuit Father Nentvig wrote. The good father, nonetheless, failed to tell of the abandoned and flooded shafts where only bones revealed the fate of a hungry miner. Almost as important as mining in Sonora was livestock breeding. In the 1880s noted author Adolph F. Bandelier listed in his journals: "1200 souls, 2000 cattle in Huassavas [*sic*], and 600 souls, 7000–8000 cattle in Granados." The fame of the Sonoran mules reached as far away as Mexico City. Sonoran brands appeared in Santa Fe, many hundreds of leagues to the north. Knowledge of the mule trade would later become an important component of the business world of Tules and her older brother, Trinidad.[23] Mules pulled the wagonloads of merchandise that flowed across the Chihuahua and Santa Fe Trails.

Once trade with the United States began with the opening of the Santa Fe Trail in 1821, traders routinely sold their Mexican mules after arriving in Missouri. It was necessary for Mexican *arrieros*, or muleteers, to accompany the wild mules. In 1843 some twelve hundred mules crossed the Santa Fe Trail in a single wagon train bound for Independence, where they were herded aboard a steamboat bound for St. Louis.[24] These wild mules bit viciously and proved to be more dangerous than bulls bred for the bullrings. Mules were the most profitable of all Mexican animals and the most desirable for long journeys of a thousand miles because of their endurance. They carried four or five hundred pounds while averaging thirteen miles per day.[25]

Members of the Barceló family continued to be among the foremost cattle ranchers of Sonora. In the year 1963, at least eighty-five brands still existed under that name alone. Contemporary Barcelós play a significant role in the cattle industry and its political organization in the state of Sonora.[26]

The decision of the Juan Ignacio Barcelós to abandon Sonora for New Mexico can be attributed in part, if not entirely, to the vulnerable frontier life in Huásabas and Granados. From time to time, trade caravans passed through the Sonoran and Bavispe valleys carrying products from far northern New Spain to central Mexico. Traveling merchants told vivid stories from the vast land to the north, land which still belonged to the Spanish empire and would until 1821. As early as 1804, mining began near Santa Rita in southern New Mexico, and the New Mexico's wealth reached Sonora. Added to the Indian turmoil were word-of-mouth assurances that once the separation from Spain occurred, lucrative trade between Mexico and the United States would begin. Rumors of the gold discovery in the mountains south of Santa Fe may have filtered down the trail as well. The temptation to leave Sonora appeared irresistible.

Around the year of 1815 the Juan Ignacio Barcelós of east-central Sonora began a long and arduous journey to the most northern sector of New Spain to seek a new and better life. The ensuing year was known as "the year without a summer" due to the April volcanic eruption of Mount Tambora in distant Indonesia. Under a haze of ash the Barceló family may have traveled and lived for a time. Climatic cooling caused by the volcanic explosion might have adversely affected agricultural growth in Sonora and northern New Spain. Some historical accounts even attribute the failure of Thomas Jefferson's crops at Monticello to the lingering ash blocking the sun's rays.

Whether the earth-encircling ash or the Apache raids prompted their departure from Sonora, the Barcelós packed their belongings into one or more mule-drawn carts, whereupon they joined another large caravan of traders and soldiers for protection of livestock on the dry *jornadas* where Apaches and Comanches lurked.[27] As a precocious teenager, Gertrudis Barceló must have looked on this trip as the greatest adventure of her young and unfulfilled life. What she could not know, but perhaps secretly yearned for, was that with her arrival in New Spain she would play a legendary role in the pages of nineteenth-century New Mexico history. Because of the international trade on the Chihuahua and Santa Fe Trails her fame became worldwide.

CHAPTER TWO

Valencia and Real de Dolores

~⁀

For reasons unknown, Juan Ignacio Barceló and his family chose the bucolic village of Valencia south of Albuquerque as their new home in 1815. Once settled on the Río Grande they found the valley to be as fertile as the Bavispe Valley in Sonora for the cultivation of grapes and the pursuit of farming and ranching.[1] The Barcelós lived on the main artery of El Camino Real de Tierra Adentro from Santa Fe to Chihuahua and central Mexico.

News from north and south flowed through the village with every passing caravan or mail carrier. In 1822 Tomé and Santa Fe were the sole post offices and distribution points for the fifty-four surrounding settlements of northern New Mexico.[2] The Camino Real was the long and treacherous road leading to and from the interior known as Nueva España, New Spain, a distant place that had sorely disappointed sixteenth-century *conquistadores* searching for riches. Despite a seemingly tranquil existence in Valencia, the same dreaded Indian menace that had plagued the lives of Juan Ignacio's family in Sonora again lurked as a threat.

A decade before the arrival of the Barcelós in Valencia, Lieutenant Zebulon Montgomery Pike met a troop of Spanish soldiers on a reconnaissance in the San Luis Valley of today's southern Colorado in 1806.[3] They informed him that he indeed was not on the Red River as he believed but rather the Río Grande, and he was dangerously trespassing on Spanish soil. The "Lost Pathfinder" failed to climb the mountain named for him today, Pikes Peak.[4] The Americans were taken to Santa Fe, where Zebulon Pike described the town's church steeples towering over the low-lying and "miserable" mud houses. Displaying true New Mexican hospitality, colonial officials wined and dined Lieutenant Pike and his men before escorting them down El Camino Real to Chihuahua for interrogation under the supervision of Spanish officer Facundo Melgares, who became New Mexico's last colonial governor from 1818 to 1822.

On the outskirts of Albuquerque, the *estranjeros*, or foreigners, met Lieutenant Melgares, who, according to Pike, possessed the urbanity of a Frenchman rather than the haughtiness of a Castilian. Melgares dispatched an order to the surrounding villages, of which Valencia was one, to parade their "handsomest young girls" at a fandango, or *baile*, which he sponsored. As a military officer who also appreciated the cordial Hispanic women in their loose, low-cut blouses, short skirts, and no apparent stockings or drawers, Pike accepted the invitation to attend the ball, noting an impressive "display of beauty."[5] Living on the Camino Real offered opportunities to meet strange men, hear their many different languages, and enjoy the political gossip from Santa Fe.

Lieutenant Pike estimated the population of Santa Fe in 1807 to be forty-five hundred souls, more than 10 percent of the total New Mexican population.[6] The general ethnic mix of New Mexico eleven years later in 1818 consisted of "free whites and civilized Indians, a very few European Spaniards, and absolutely no negro souls," according to one early account.[7] Based on official reports, the provincial population by 1822 was about forty thousand. These people were generally poor, polite, and pleasure-loving; there was virtually no industry and little commerce, circumstances that would dramatically change with the opening of trade on the Santa Fe Trail. The main arena of commerce was the noisy hustle and bustle of local markets, conducted mainly in Spanish. The little merchandise that arrived in New Mexico came by way of the province of Sonora, contraband introduced by the English via the Gulf of California.

According to the account of Amado Chaves of the Río Abajo (the "lower river," that is, the part of New Mexico lying along of the Río Grande below Santa Fe), the Barcelós lived in an old hacienda in Valencia belonging to his grandfather, Manuel Antonio Chaves.[8] The names of Juan Ignacio Barceló and María Dolores Herrero first appear as *padrinos*, or godparents, in Catholic church records of May 1816.[9] Thereafter, the couple served as spiritual grandparents, or padrinos and *madrinas*, to a number of babies born to friends and neighbors in the neighboring villages of Valencia and Tomé.[10] By July 1820, however, Juan Ignacio's name disappears from New Mexico records. His death is unrecorded, which perhaps indicates rather ironically that after surviving numerous Apache raids in Sonora he may have been killed by hostile Apaches or Navajos in his newly adopted homeland.[11]

In its prime, Tomé, the neighboring settlement immediately south of Valencia, was a prosperous town whose center included a plaza where annual festivals attracted hundreds of people who reveled and prayed for days on end. And so it had continued until the Indian attacks began. In 1776 people were killed or carried away into captivity, the beginning of Tomé's decline into semiabandonment, the haciendas no longer filled with activity or laughter.[12] There was no escaping Indian incursions after leaving Sonora, but the Indian attacks now came either from the northwest or from the eastern plains known as the Llano Estacado, or staked plains.

An agricultural and wine-producing area in the central Río Grande Valley, Valencia and Tomé received their agonizing share of abductions and deaths. Disease among infants took its toll as well. Death withstanding, solace could be found in the teachings of the Catholic Church, which greatly influenced the lives of early New Mexicans. And were it not for nineteenth-century church records, albeit some of which are unfortunately missing, this story could not be told in its fullest.

Approximately eight years after her arrival in Valencia as a teenager, Gertrudis Barceló married Manuel Antonio Sisneros, a descendant of Antonio Cisneros, who returned to northern New Mexico in 1693 from El Paso following the Pueblo Indian Revolt of 1680.[13] The twenty-one-year-old groom, born in the Plaza de San Rafael north of Santa Fe (Alcalde), was the son of Hermenegildo Cisneros and his second wife, María Rita Lucero, who was the daughter of Salvador Manuel Lucero de Godoy, an old Río Arriba (upriver) family from north of Santa Fe.[14] In 1829 the then-widowed María Rita and members of her family lived in the village of Manzano, east of Albuquerque, following her marriage to Tomás Sanches of Río Abajo. Here the Sisneros family married into well-known Abajo families such as the Archuletas, Barcelós, Cháveses, Labadies, and Sancheses.[15]

Unlike her American contemporaries on the Atlantic coast but similar to her contemporaries in Latin America and Spain, a nineteenth-century New Mexican woman retained her maiden name, property, and legal rights after marriage, along with her wages. She also retained her sexual urges. No submissive double standard existed whereby her husband dominated her body and soul. Nor were these independent women excluded from men's work in the fields, as the American officer Zebulon M. Pike observed. These proud women and girls protected their complexions against the burning sun and dryness with a crimson juice called *alegría*, mixed with clay and starch.[16]

Twenty-three-year-old María Gertrudis Barceló married Manuel Antonio Sisneros in 1823, two years following the opening of the Santa Fe Trail to Kansas and Missouri.[17] Marriage, pregnancy, childbirth, and infant death consumed the ensuing life of the adult Tules, who was already four months pregnant at the time of her marriage on June 20, 1823. A son, José Pedro Sisneros, baptized October 19, 1823, lived for one month only. A second son, Miguel Antonio Sisneros, baptized January 9, 1825, died at age four months.[18] The exact cause of their deaths remains unknown. Epidemics of infectious diseases struck Hispanics living in the Río Abajo of central New Mexico during the second half of the nineteenth century and the early twentieth century. Church baptismal records reveal the high mortality due to smallpox, diphtheria, measles, influenza, and pertussis in the surrounding areas near the community of Tomé. In 1826 the airborne microorganisms claimed at least one-third of the population of Valencia. One or more of these diseases probably caused the unfortunate deaths of the two infant sons of Gertrudis Barceló and Manuel Antonio Sisneros.[19]

The disappointment of unfulfilled motherhood apparently played a decisive role in Tules's restless life for the next few years. With a strong maternal desire she yearned for a family of her own, which ultimately proved to be an extended family of adopted girls, perhaps indicative of her protective nature. A year after the death of their second son, Tules and Manuel Antonio served as padrinos in Tomé in March 1826 at the birth of María del Refugio, who was born to *padres no conocidos*, or parents unknown.[20] Refugio became the adopted daughter of Tules and Manuel Antonio. For the next fifteen years, or until her marriage in 1841 to a Mexican trader, the adopted Refugio lived in the Gertrudis Barceló household.[21]

As Tules stood on the threshold of her twenty-year career as a reputed prostitute, renowned gambler, and shrewd businesswoman, she was surely influenced by the counsel of her priest, the secular Don Francisco Ignacio de Madariaga, a native of Chihuahua who had arrived in Tomé in 1821.[22] He may have wisely perceived that Tules was about to stray from the arms of the church. Madariaga held what today might be called revivals for members of his flock, focusing predominantly on women who were living outside the bonds of holy matrimony or who indulged in prostitution. Quite likely, however, the priest had never encountered a strong-willed woman such as the enterprising Tules, whose prayers surely included those directed to San Cayetano, patron saint of gambling. Francisco Ignacio de Madariaga died in 1838 before Doña Tules had reached the pinnacle of her career in the 1840s.[23]

From the pain and disappointment of two unsuccessful births tempered with the consoling adoption of a baby girl in 1826, Gertrudis Barceló quickly focused on an exciting venture in a new place, where her exceptional gift of gambling might garner great wealth. Along with her new motherhood, Tules began in earnest to also test her luck with cards and men. The protection of a male companion was a necessity for the woman gambler who kept her winnings close by her side. Thus the year between 1825 and 1826 may be said to mark the documented beginning of the professional gambling career of the celebrated Gertrudis Barceló in the hills south of Santa Fe.

The remote mining camp known as Oso Springs or Oro (prior to 1831) or subsequently as Real de Dolores was nestled in the Ortíz Mountains twenty-six miles from Santa Fe, where gold and boredom supplied a card game with a captive audience of disheveled and miserable miners called *gambucinos*. Little known at the time, but historically predating the famous California gold rush of 1849 by at least twenty-five years, Real de Dolores was the first major gold rush in what is today the western United States. Few people today know about this isolated site south of Santa Fe. It is thought to be the best preserved mining camp of the Mexican Period (1821–46) in the Southwest.[24]

Mountainous gold regions were considered to be communal property developed by hungry indigents on their own hook. Often surviving on one or two *reales* per day when times were hard, an early Dolores miner lived on a meager diet of bread, ranchero cheese if available, and a *piloncillo*, or coarse cake of sugar.[25] The shortage of water for the gold washers meant that winter was the preferred season of their operations. By the 1830s prominent New Mexican Rafael Chacón recalled that after the harvesting of the crops it was customary to travel to the old placer or Real de Dolores in winter.[26]

Doña Tules may have commuted from Valencia or Santa Fe to Real

FIGURE 3. ❧ Real de Dolores, New Mexico, ca. 1894. Author's collection.

de Dolores during the wet months, when the rush of miners increased the population to its greatest extent. The Real challenged Santa Fe for population from the early 1820s to 1839 until the opening of Real del Tuerto, when thousands thronged to that area.[27]

In the 1830s a motley assemblage of gamblers, cardsharps, and miners consumed large quantities of food—flour, cornmeal, and fattened and dressed pigs—brought by the ever assiduous Don Rafael Paiz, Rafael Chacón's father-in-law, who had profited by several hundred dollars at the end of each year. Meals cost twenty-five cents each; baked goods and fritters at a hefty fifty cents a dozen warmed the cold evening hours, accompanied by the singing of improvised *cuandos* or *décimas*, a lost art today.[28] Such luxuries may not have been available when Gertrudis Barceló dealt monte to miners and merchants. Ultimately, because of the scarcity of water, the placers were never truly successful. Peak gold production came during 1832–35, when the woman gambler named Barceló was found living in Santa Fe.[29]

Coincidentally, the arrival in Real de Dolores of Gertrudis Barceló, one of the first and best known of its residents, proves to be the earliest documented period of the name of the small, isolated real near Santa Fe. A Doctor Willard of St. Charles, Missouri, traveling to New Mexico in 1825 with trader Augustus Storrs, wrote, "The mines in the neighborhood of Santa Fe were formerly worked but are now abandoned," perhaps meaning the silver mining area.[30] Author Josiah Gregg noted the year of 1828 as the legendary discovery of gold by a Sonoreño mule herder. Questionable myths abound about any gold discovery and its exact date.[31]

In 1824 a trading party from St. Louis returned with $180,000 in gold and $10,000 in furs, leading us to believe that the Real de Dolores gold discovery dates at least four years earlier than recorded by Josiah Gregg.[32] Gregg further comments that the placer mining fever, which he dates from 1828 as stated, caused excitement in the area. And even though the first two or three years of production proved insignificant, the purity of the gold was found to be extraordinary—at least $19.70 or $20 to the troy ounce. Later, and with the relatively brief assistance of Spaniard Dámaso López, gold production between 1826 to 1845 in the Ortíz Mountains may have reached $1 million.[33]

Gold nuggets or dust not gambled away filled the pockets of small

storekeepers, who *vendar los ojos*—hookwinked the remote miners—
into paying inflated prices for their food and supplies. Add to the inflated
prices the customary practice of Mexican merchants and American
traders to discount the mint price of gold from twenty dollars per ounce
to sixteen dollars, a 20 percent profit as "carrying charges."[34] Meanwhile,
Santa Feans kept their avaricious eyes on the fast-moving rush of gold
and gambling south of Santa Fe. In 1826 Juan Vigil y Martínez, the *teniente de justica* of Real del Oro, fined Gertrudis Barceló forty-three pesos
for gaming, then prohibited due to the Spanish *bandos*, or decrees, issued
as early as 1703 to prohibit gaming by civilians and soldiers alike.[35]

Manuel Antonio Sisneros, husband of Tules, also paid gambling
fines.[36] A *diligencia*, or kickback, was taken by Vigil y Martínez, or so
Administrator de Rentas Juan Bautista Vigil y Alarid discovered in 1826.
The greedy teniente, later *alcalde*, or magistrate, had pocketed twenty-
one pesos of the forty-three peso fine, almost a 50-percent commission. Because of the low salaries paid to officials by the Spanish colonial
authorities, *mordidas*, literally meaning "bites," were a system of remu-
neration practiced by the Mexicans.[37] How long Doña Tules had been
gambling in Real de Dolores prior to her fine has not been established,
nor is it known if she was the only woman gambler. Not surprisingly, the
oldest profession known to man, prostitution, which flourished in all
mining camps, established itself quickly in the camps near Santa Fe.

In Spanish colonial days a *tribunal de vagos*, or special court, was
established to deal with vagabonds or those without an appropriate
employment, including women. Two prostitutes were held in the Real
del Oro jail in 1835. Considered illegal and seldom discussed in documents, prostitution or fornication existed, nevertheless. One prostitute
had run away to New Mexico from the Mexican interior to escape her
husband. The tribunal rendered a judgment that she should be returned
to Mexico or else kept in a reputable house until her mother came to
take her home.[38]

The puritanical Josiah Gregg noted that between the years 1832 and
1835 the amount of gold extracted at Real de Dolores was at least $60,000
to $80,000 per annum, then a great sum of money. In 1838 Gregg trav-
eled the Santa Fe Trail eastward to Missouri with a train of seven wagons
carrying $150,000 in bullion, proceeds of the previous year's profits for
the Chihuahua traders.[39]

The placer mines produced nuggets or gold dust. Anticipating the diminishing ore panned or extracted by the gambling miners, Tules appears to have remained in Real de Dolores a fairly short time. She had only begun to master the political maneuvering of Santa Fe officials, who controlled her chosen pursuit. The card game of monte, a game of pure chance and deception, was considered the national obsession of Mexicans. As a young girl in Sonora, Tules surely watched or pitched a *quartilla* or two (one and one-quarter cents each), later banking and dealing in the game of monte, the game that became the hallmark of her many skills.[40]

Josiah Gregg related: "Some twelve or fifteen years ago there lived (or rather roamed) in Taos a certain female of very loose habits, known as *La Tules*. Finding it difficult to obtain the means of living in that district, she finally extended her wanderings to the capital."[41] This derogatory account is refuted by Mexican War correspondent Richard Smith Elliott, who in 1847 wrote, "Gregg is wrong as to her having 'roved in the valley of Taos,' confounding her sister-in-law, *La Senora Dona Doloxes* [*sic*] *Barcelo*, with Tules."[42] I believe this analysis by correspondent Elliott to be correct, although Tules may have gambled from time to time during the early 1830s in Taos with Dolores Griego, wife of Tules's brother Trinidad.[43]

Concerning this long-standing confusion of names in New Mexico history of Dolores Barceló and Dolores Griego, Gertrudis, and Tules, a Mexican *dicho*, or saying, with a *doble sentido del lenguaje*, or double entendre, seems rather appropriate. It warns that "él que se acuesta con tules, amanece con dolores," literally meaning "he who lies down with reeds awakens with pains" or "he who lies down with Gertrudis awakens with Dolores." More explanation is that "esto es lo escrito, pero el refrán es un tantcuanto equívoco por la existencia en él de dos nombres de mujer: Dolores y Tules, sinónimo éste de Gertrudis"—"It is also written, that the refrain is for the confounding existence of two women's names: Dolores and Tules, synonymous with Gertrudis."[44]

Tules, her mother Dolores, her adopted daughter Refugio, and husband Manuel Antonio lived in Santa Fe by June 1, 1833, or possibly even a year earlier.[45] The fame and popularity of Doña Gertrudis Barceló as a *madrina* to newborns paralleled her rise as a shrewd monte dealer and successful business woman. Her name appeared in the Tomé and

Santa Fe marriage, baptism, and burial records at least twenty-one times between 1833 and 1852.[46]

A short time after the first of two ill-fated births to Tules, her widowed mother, Dolores Herrero, married a Don Pedro Pino on August 6, 1823. Pino was a forty-year-old native of Los Chaves in the Belén parish, who was then living in Valencia.[47] Until the mother's name appeared in Santa Fe church documents in 1832, her interim whereabouts remain unknown. Dolores Herrero y Barceló de Pino lived in Santa Fe until 1841.[48] The second husband of Dolores Herrero de Barceló may be either an adopted son or relative of the renowned Pedro Bautista Pino, who in 1810 was elected to represent New Mexico, still a part of Spain, at the Cortes, the Spanish representative body that assembled in Cadíz to draft a Spanish constitution.[49] Pedro Bautista Pino was elected a delegate a second time to attend the Cortes of 1820–21. During this time Mexico stood on the brink of severing its ties with Spain, and Pino was forced to return for lack of funds, thus inspiring the apt couplet, "Don Pedro Pino fué, Don Pedro Pino vino"—"Don Pedro went, Don Pedro Pino came." Pedro Bautista Pino died on April 19, 1829, leaving his beloved New Mexico forever.[50]

In the early 1820s, placer mining in New Mexico first emerged as a significant industry in the Placer Viejo, or Old Placer, of the Ortíz Mountains south of Santa Fe. Large gold shipments crossed the Santa Fe Trail eastward to Missouri, totaling about three-quarters of a million dollars from Real de Dolores production alone during the twenty-year gambling career of Doña Tules. It may thus be concluded that Real de Dolores gold largely financed Santa Fe Trail trade. Not only gold but shipments of silver from Chihuahua bound for Missouri crossed the dangerous Jornada del Muerto northward to reach Santa Fe before turning eastward to travel the Santa Fe Trail after 1821, the opening of trade.

One poorly protected and therefore risky trip in Chihuahua in October 1835 to the village of Jesús-María, consisting of but one American and a Mexican muleteer with three or four mules, is narrated by Josiah Gregg.[51] Transportation of the heavy specie required special packaging in sacks made of wet, raw buffalo and beef hides, which shrank when dried. These tightly stitched bags of coins contained from one to two thousand dollars per muleload and were compressed tightly to prevent friction.[52] One misstep by the usually surefooted animal while descending a narrow trail from a mine could send money and animal over the edge of any precipice.

Not until the early 1840s can evidence of any possible involvement by Doña Tules in the specie trade on the Santa Fe Trail be found.[53] The American James M. Giddings, originally from Missouri, arrived in Santa Fe sometime in the 1830s. He was yet to marry another adopted daughter of Doña Tules named Petra Gutierres.[54] Whether Giddings had earlier earned Tules's trust with large sums of money remains questionable. Nevertheless, it was in the spring of 1841 that a caravan set out from Santa Fe for Missouri carrying $180,000 to $200,000 in specie in twenty-two wagons. Traders traveling in this caravan were "Messrs. Giddings, from Fayette, McGuffin [James W. Magoffin], Garvis [Chaves] and some other Spanish gentlemen" who reached Independence, Missouri.[55] It seems likely that some of the specie belonged to Gertrudis Barceló. Never known to have left New Mexico to travel to Missouri, Tules was forced to entrust her money with her friend, gambling partner, and future son-in-law, James Giddings.

The bilingual sons-in-law of Tules became reliable couriers on both the Chihuahua and Santa Fe trails. The gambler may have traveled to Durango, Zacatecas, or San Juan de los Lagos to gamble at Mexican fairs with Santiago Flores, husband of Tules's adopted daughter Refugio.[56] A family affair, mothers-in-law, wives, and families of traders crossed the trails, though few are documented. Church baptismal records show that in the 1840s María Refugio Flores traveled with her husband, giving birth to several babies in Santa Fe and at least one child in Chihuahua.[57]

In September 1841 Santiago Flores moved southward down the Camino Real carrying fifty *tercios*, or muleload bales, of domestic merchandise with a value of 297 pesos and 6 reales.[58] Again in 1844 he traveled to Chihuahua, Durango, and Moctezuma in Sonora with a combined cargo of sixty-four and more *bultos* (bundles) carrying a value of more than 6,700 pesos. Making at least four trips, Flores returned to New Mexico from Moctezuma in 1845 with fifty-five bultos of domestic merchandise and 900 pesos *en dinero* (in cash).[59]

In May 1843 a caravan from Santa Fe, composed largely of Mexican traders, forty-two wagons, and twelve hundred mules, arrived in Independence. The group had avoided Texan Charles A. Warfield's marauders by traveling the lower trace or Cimarron Cutoff of the Santa Fe Trail.

Leaving Santa Fe around April 1 the principal traders reached St. Louis carrying "sixteen bales and twelve boxes of silver, reportedly totaling between $250,000 and $300,000," plus fifty packs of furs. Eleven of the traders traveled on to New York "to make purchases." Those named were José Gutierrez, John Pravis [José Chaves?], James Floris [Santiago Flores], P. Arando, "J. Olaro" [Otero?], M. Sandrue, J. C. [Juan Cristóbal?] Armijo, R. [Rafael?] Armijo, W. [H.] Glasgow, and N. W. Greene."[60] Interestingly, three students from prominent New Mexican families— Francisco Perea, Joaquin Perea, and J. Francisco Chávez—also traveled in this caravan en route to enter the Jesuit college in St. Louis.

Josiah Gregg wrote that in 1843 Doña Tules had sent ten thousand dollars across the Santa Fe Trail. Three months later, in August of the same year as the Armijo-Flores wagon train crossing, President Antonio López de Santa Anna issued a decree declaring the customs houses in northern Chihuahua, Paso del Norte (El Paso), and Taos closed to foreign trade. One year earlier in 1842 the Mexican government had also prohibited importation of fifty different articles and exportation of gold and silver bullion. The timing of the shipment of Tules's money in the Armijo-Flores caravan of 1843 may reflect prior knowledge of the impending mandate. In December 1842 she had written from Chihuahua to her onetime business associate, Mexican governor Manuel Armijo in Santa Fe, telling of her invitation to attend a reception in honor of General José Mariano Monterde, the new commanding general and governor of Chihuahua.[61] She did not attend the reception. Then, on her return to Santa Fe in early 1843, she quickly proceeded to send her money out of the country.[62]

On March 7, 1846, another caravan headed for Missouri and carrying mules and money possibly belonging to Gertrudis Barceló was raided at Cow Creek on the Santa Fe Trail by Pawnee Indians. A total of forty-four mules and two horses were stolen from Norris Colburn, Messrs. Armijo and company, which included "A. [Ambrosio] Armijo, James Flores, Mr. Elliott, and Mr. Lussard." Almost destitute of stock, the Armijo party was forced to walk two hundred miles, reaching Independence ten days later. Colburn arrived several days after the rest, carrying their luggage and 350 pounds of gold dust. He wrote from Cow Creek that the Pawnees attacked the traders, killed five Mexicans, and wounded another Mexican at Wagon Mound. Mexican traders in the

Armijo group could speak English so well that the Indians thought the Mexicans to be Americans, and thus they escaped a violent death.[63] As violent as Indian attacks might be, winter was often savage on the Santa Fe Trail; trader Santiago Flores became ill during the crossing and recovered but one of his servants died. The Armijo traders were expected to return to Santa Fe with stocks of goods in the spring.

FIGURE 4. ❧ August de Marle (left, ca. 1816–61), a lover of Doña
            Tules, and attorney Charles P. Clever (right), 1856.
            Museum of New Mexico neg. no. 7131.

At Independence, after carrying the gold dust, the trail-weary traders boarded the *Tobacco Plant*, a river steamboat, which docked at St. Louis on March 25, 1846. Some of the mules stolen at Wagon Mound and accompanied by Santiago Flores may have been owned by Doña Tules. The gambler had found New Mexico gold and Mexican mules to be a highly profitable though risky endeavor. The gold mines of New Mexico were said to have been worked with great success. When an estimated $1 million exchanged hands in trade, several hundred wagons would be required to carry it.[64]

Between May 8 and May 14 in 1846, three months prior to the arrival of the American military in Santa Fe to initiate the U.S.–Mexican War, several Chihuahua trading companies, which included trader James Magoffin and his thirty wagons, arrived in Independence, Missouri, reportedly carrying $350,000 in specie and a thousand mules. So it is quite evident from various accounts that immense amounts of specie and numbers of mules were moving from west to east.[65] Because of the lack of accurate documentation, compiling a record of ownership remains difficult.[66]

Among the rumors about Doña Tules and her alleged mining activities in New Mexico that reached St. Louis was one in 1847 following the end of the U.S.–Mexican War. It involved a second lieutenant in the American army named August de Marle. A thirty-six-year-old Prussian, de Marle joined Artillery Company B under Captain Woldemar Fischer and commanded by Colonel Sterling Price.[67] The brief newspaper notice read, "Among the many good friends and acquaintances who marched against Santa Fe more than a year ago and whose hands we could shake yesterday, we missed August de Marle. The sly fox [de Marle] has married a Mexican and wants to run her [Doña Tules's?] mines." It may have been only an offhand remark made by one of de Marle's Missouri Volunteer friends misinterpreted by O. Benckendorff, a friend of de Marle and editor of *Die Tägliche Deutsche Tribüne* (The Daily German Tribune).[68] Four months later the same St. Louis German newspaper recanted another rumor, writing, "Aug. De Marle is not married—he is, however, alcalde and draws a considerable sum annually."[69] Doña Tules surrounded herself with men of power and intellect. August de Marle was surely the most educated and brilliant of her lovers.

CHAPTER THREE

Reina de la Baraja, Queen of the Deck

⁓

Termed a "distinguishing propensity" of the Mexican people by noted author Josiah Gregg in his *Commerce of the Prairies,* gambling was a national passion that prevailed at all levels of society—the *ranchero,* the doña, the child, the domestic, and even the *pobretería,* or the poor. A governor and priest might also be seen elbowing their way through the crowd to reach the table piled high with cards, thus the name *monte,* or mountain.[1]

The game of monte was played with a forty-card Spanish deck, which contained suits of ten cards each—clubs, swords, suns, and cups; the eights, nines, and tens were omitted. The cards were numbered from ace to seven, with the jack (knave) and the horse in place of the queen and the king. The banker shuffles the deck and then takes two cards, called the layout, from the bottom of the pack and places them face up and close together on the table. The punters, or players, now bet on these two cards.[2] The dealer takes two more cards from the top of the deck and places them on the table. The punters may bet on these or any card in

FIGURE 5. ⪦ "Gambling Saloon in Santa Fe," *Harper's Monthly Magazine,*
April 1854. Museum of New Mexico neg. no. 14963.

the layout. The banker now holds the deck face upward, resulting in the
bottom card now being on top. There being four layout cards, if the card
shown on the top is the same kind, the player then receives the value of
his stake; if not, the banker wins the entire stake. As the game continues
the banker draws the cards one by one, until all the cards are out, which
concludes a deal. At this point, a punter may bet as much as he or she
wishes against the bank, limited only by the amount in the bank.[3]

There was a time when one hundred monte tables operated in
Santa Fe, and the capitalization of the bank amounted to one thousand dollars.[4] Monte was considered a *juego prohibido,* or illegal game,
controlled by fines that fed the municipal coffers of Santa Fe. By 1838
gamblers' fines became fees, but the gaming nonetheless teetered on the
brink of illegality. Legal or not, gambling was a moneymaker for town
officials. Governor Manuel Armijo quickly saw the money to be reaped

by making gambling legal. In April 1849 gaming licenses in Santa Fe County contributed $1,750 to the treasury, while dram shops (saloons) contributed only $1,256.66.[5]

Games of monte varied from the use of the full deck of forty Spanish cards to three-card monte. One veteran gambler confessed that there was no honest dealer of three-card monte—the game was conceived as a swindle from the start. Every monte dealer knew that if the cards were thrown fairly, even the dullest player was able to follow the right card— no matter how fast the cards were thrown. The monte dealer must cheat to make it any kind of game at all. And a word of advice—no monte dealer on the street entered the business without immediate protection nearby. Manuel Antonio Sisneros, husband of Doña Tules, gambled and protected her in the early days of her career in the 1820s and 1830s.[6] Following his abrupt disappearance after 1841, however, American James Madison Giddings and Mexican Santiago Flores became lookouts and guards for the monte-dealing Tules, often dealing the cards for her. After 1846 the scholarly Prussian August de Marle became her dealer, protector, and lover, following the arrival of the American army.[7]

It has been said that after the arrival of the U.S. Army and until the Civil War in the 1860s, the stakes appeared to be much larger than in the past. As early as the 1840s a staggering forty-thousand-dollar stake was observed to be "covered" and a ten-thousand-dollar stake, often changing hands in ten minutes, wasn't even worth mentioning among the gossipmongers of Santa Fe.[8] During his lifetime in nineteenth- and twentieth-century New Mexico, the affable Abe Spiegelberg, a cousin of the well-known Spiegelberg Brothers, early Jewish Santa Fe and Chihuahua Trail merchants, recalled seeing men "win $50,000 on one turn of faro."[9] Nickels ultimately replaced dollars on the gaming tables after the turn of the century. By the time the old Fonda became the Exchange Hotel and met its demise by demolition via a World War I tank to benefit the sale of U.S. war bonds in 1913, the high-flying days of the Chihuahua and Santa Fe trails had long ended, the monte tables a distant memory.

Gertrudis Barceló, raised in a Sonoran society whose time was spent gambling, horse racing, and cockfighting, observed the paucity of labor during her childhood. She surely decided that as an adult there might be a faster though not necessarily easier way to achieve wealth. A hint of fearful awe prevailed in the diaries of many men who visited Santa Fe and described the ability of the renowned Santa Fe gambler. Tules possessed an "eye of shrewd intelligence with an expression of mischievous bright-ness. . . . Her figure was neat, her manners free and not ungraceful as she waltzed."[10] Strangers and prominent Santa Feans "had been stripped of accumulated property."[11] The substantial amount of real estate that Doña Tules acquired must have resulted from her gambling expertise.

Tules probably acquired little formal education as a young girl. Nevertheless, American army officers were quick to criticize and fall victim to her gambling acumen. In 1846 Lieutenant J. F. Gilmer of the U.S. Corps of Engineers wrote: "The leader of society among the ladies! of Santa Fe is an elderly Señora of the name of Toulis, who was born and educated in Taos. In early life, she went in company with some American trad-ers to Chihuahua, afterwards to Durango, where she acquired wealth by playing at monte, which has been increased by keeping a monte Bank since. She now lives in good style, and is one of the *elite* in the society of Santa Fe."[12]

Many accounts written by those visiting Santa Fe have the ring of dubious hearsay rather than actual fact. Prominent Santa Fe merchant and diplomat Manuel Alvarez, nevertheless, sheds new light on the fas-cinating woman, who, with James Giddings in 1850, owed him $150 at the rate of 2 percent interest per month, a substantial 24 percent per year.[13] The suspicious Alvarez questioned her gambling honesty. For example, Alvarez seemed convinced that Doña Tules practiced the art of phrenology in order to predict her opponents' behavioral char-acteristics, thus a logical reasoning, at least to Alvarez, for her unpar-alleled success.[14] Having lost money to Tules by gaming or otherwise, and in apparent frustration, the acerbic Alvarez scribbled the follow-ing observation: "She [Tules] has (though I doubt that she ever studied Phrinologie [phrenology]) the keenest eye for perceiving the existence of certain bumps and the absence of some others on the heads of indi-viduals from which talent she derives all her great advantages."[15]

As noted earlier, monte was the chosen game of the famous Doña Tules. She dealt night after night, often until dawn, with "skilful preci-sion" as the cards "slipped from her long fingers as steadily as though she were handling only a knitting needle."[16] With feminine bravado, Tules's deft and beringed fingers swept away piles of gold, the result of perpetual practice, as she won time and again. Opponents who nervously fingered their cards seemed almost mesmerized with the unflappable woman gambler, who may or may not have smoked a *cigarrito* as she played. "Her neck was adorned with three heavy chains of gold, to the longest of which was attached a massive crucifix of the same precious metal."[17] Wearing a loose-fitting dress while gambling allowed her a certain degree of comfort after sitting for many hours on end, often until morning.[18] A soberness and an occasional faint curling of a smile covered Tules's countenance as the monte game continued until she or her opponent won or lost. "Yes, pour them [the gold coins] out, old lady. . . . Pour the yellow rascals out; we may as well make one job of it before morning," a brash Kentucky trader taunted the woman monte dealer after taking a bolstering swig of Pass whiskey.[19] When winning, another spectator noted that "her keen black eyes seem about to start from their sockets . . . when losing, a melancholy smile flickered across her wrinkled countenance."[20] The game finally ended. As her opponent was leaving dead broke, he danced a tipsy jig around the room yelling, "Wake snakes! Hail Columbia! I'm off for California to-morrow! And, I say, old lady, I'll see you again in the fall."[21] With a curtsey and commanding demeanor, the graceful Tules swiftly exited through a side door with her companions, disappearing into the dawn.[22]

The game of monte withstanding, *chuza* was the game of choice for many "respectable ladies" of New Mexico who flocked to the roulette-type wheel day and night until their obsessed faces and sunken eyes revealed that the "excitement was too powerful for their systems."[23] During the nineteenth century, Santa Fe carpenters were kept busy supplying the demand for chuza tables; a few still exist today in museum collections. Tables operated at various locations throughout the town as late as the 1870s.[24]

In 1846, when gambling competition was fierce, a U.S. soldier named Philip Gooch Ferguson estimated that there were more than one hundred monte tables in Santa Fe. Other popular games among New Mexicans were faro, brag (played in Chihuahua), poker, canute, and among U.S. soldiers, seven-up (a type of fan-tan), high-low-jack, honest John, and blackjack, with the most popular being studhorse and draw poker. Carcaman involved the toss of dice to decide the lucky number in a raffle. Army barrack stakes included socks, drawers, trousers, buttons, and other items of wearing apparel auctioned off by quartermaster stores.[25]

The obsession for gambling in New Mexico was not limited to any one ethnic group, however. An American soldier commented, "It may not be credited, but I saw a Jew betting on monte, and I am told he is a constant frequenter of the tables and generally wins. He seemed to bet liberally and to throw out his gold like a most accomplished black-leg [card swindler]."[26] All became professional gamblers, there being no particular stigma attached to the vice. The demon of chance and greed possessed the innocents who were known to stake their rebozos, jewelry, and who knows what else, often returning home to retrieve whatever stash remained behind the fireplace or buried in the mud floor of their *casa*.

Before silver dollars dominated the gaming tables and an American Protestant minister preached antislavery in the haunts of the sinners in 1851, each monte dealer needed to know the exchange rate of the various currencies. In July 1844, prior to the arrival of the Americans two years later, the following money could be found circulating in Santa Fe: "silver bullion, Mexican doubleloons [*sic*], quarter eagles, gold dust, Mexican dollars, hammerd [*sic*] dollars, counterfets [*sic*], and thalers."[27] A fist-sized pouch of gold nuggets and dust weighed a solid ten pounds.[28] The *Santa Fe Weekly Gazette* alerted the public to Santa Fe's lost and found in the apparent expectation of it being returned: "100 Dollars Reward. Lost at the Exchange or somewhere in the Plaza on Thurs. nite the 16th instant a small bag containing seven hundred and twenty dollars in Gold coin. . . . Charles Beaubien."[29]

Stacks of *pesos fuertes*, or Mexican dollars; French five francs; twenty- and ten-dollar gold pieces; and the notorious California fifty-dollar and eight-cornered gold slugs, a later coin of the gaming world, covered the monte and faro tables. Christopher "Kit" Carson surely took his turn at the tables and at some time may have challenged the famous Doña at monte. Antoine Robidoux, the tall and slender French-Canadian trapper from St. Louis, Missouri, who became an interpreter for the Army of the West in 1846, frequented the tables. Lesser known Santa Fe gamblers included Tules's Presbyterian neighbor "Squire" James L. Collins, interpreter for Doniphan, and Charles Thayer, a miner and gambler.[30]

As the following document corroborates, legal and counterfeit

specie from New Mexico exchanged hands in Missouri only to credit
New York accounts:

> An account of money left with me by John McNight [McKnight]
> to be forwarded to Peter Harmony & Co. of New York and by
> them placed to the credit of Mariano Lisawa [Manuel Lisa] of
> Santa Fe New Mexico. . . . [The amount] less seven dollars paid
> charges for transporting the same from Santa Fe to this place.
> July 1st 1844
>
> > Signed Duplicates
> > Saml. C. Owens [31]

The sporting woman known as La Tules wisely learned to know
the deadbeats at the monte table. On August 30, 1839, Tules took James
"Santiago" Kirker before the alcalde, claiming he owed her four hundred
pesos which she had won in a game.[32] Called a distinguished mountain-
eer and Indian slaver, Irish American Kirker opened a hotel in Santa
Fe not far from the Burro Alley gambling sala of Doña Tules.[33] In a
brief matter of minutes, as the Doña well knew, the recklessly competi-
tive traders and monte players were prone to gamble away months of
hard-earned profits from traveling the trail or herding sheep. With his
dusty Mora, New Mexico, pockets bulging with money, Colonel Cerán
St. Vrain left the area and traveled to New York to retire from the rigors
of Southwest life. He quickly returned, however, vowing never to leave
again.[34] Men such as St. Vrain and Charles E. Kearney of the prominent
St. Louis family composed the sporting fraternity of respected gamblers
who were always the most generous. They were not unlike Doña Tules
in their benevolent contributions to worthy causes.[35]

A woman openly gambling and owning her own sala was astonish-
ing to visiting American traders. Despite the condemnation found in letters and diaries written by strangers, Tules's daring behavior invariably
attracted their attention and description. In March 1847 Dr. J. M. Dunlap
wrote in his journal that in addition to compulsive gambling, "syphilis
is no means infrequent. . . . The notorious Madame Toolay nightly dis-
plays her glittering piles of gold and silver at Monte. . . . It is amusing to
observe her maneuvers during the progress of the game." Medical doctor
Dunlap also observed that women "far gone in pregnancy" attended and

took part in the many fandangos often held in the gambling places—"a child was actually born in a ballroom."[36]

The names of Gertrudis Barceló and Manuel Sisneros first appeared in Santa Fe as godparents in June of 1833.[37] Coincidentally, an Anglo American couple named Mary and William Donoho and their nine-month-old daughter arrive in Santa Fe later that same summer after crossing the Santa Fe Trail.[38] The Donohos first put down New Mexico roots by operating the old Fonda on the plaza from 1833 to 1837; it was later known as the Exchange Hotel. Whether the two redheads Mary Donoho and María Gertrudis Barceló ever encountered one another remains unknown.[39] Tules was known, however, to have gambled at Santa Fe's few hotels.

Church records indicate that María Guadalupe de Altagracia, parents unknown, was baptized on December 22, 1832, in the house of "Da. Dolores Barselo" in Santa Fe.[40] This baptismal entry indicates that Tules has moved with her mother to Santa Fe, where she lived for the remaining twenty years of her life. Godparents of María Guadalupe de Altagracia were Romualdo Sánches, son of María de la Luz Barceló (sister of Tules), and Rafaela Pino of Valencia. Rafaela, apparently yet to move to Santa Fe in 1833 from Valencia south of Albuquerque, lived for nineteen years with Tules as a servant. She may have been a relative of the Pedro Pino who married the widow Dolores Herrero de Barceló. Rafaela Pino died in Santa Fe in April 1851.[41]

Three years later, in 1836, Gertrudis is recorded on the Juan Bautista Vigil y Alarid map of Santa Fe residents.[42] She and her mother Dolores lived at numbers thirty-six and thirty-seven on the Calle de la Muralla and were neighbors of her well-educated confidante, Antonio Sena, who lived nearby at number thirty-four. Five years later, the names of Gertrudis Barceló and Manuel Sisneros appear on the 1841 Santa Fe census, their ages given as forty-one and thirty-seven years, respectively, living in the Barrio Torreón. Despite the seeming address change from Calle de la Muralla to Barrio Torreón on the census, Tules had not moved. Indeed, Calle Muralla was a part of the Barrio Torreón district. Heretofore incorrectly described by later historians and cartographers, Calle de la Muralla, *muralla* meaning wall, wrapped around the presidio, presently the Palace of the Governors, on the east, north, and west sides in 1836 and 1841.[43] On the Vigil y Alarid list the name of

Dolores Barceló (the mother) is now missing, indicating that she has died sometime after 1841.

Doña Tules first began to accumulate her wealth with the gold that came from Real de Dolores. As Santa Fe Trail traders began to arrive into New Mexico, the gold shipments flowed eastward to specie-starved Missouri. An astute Tules became aware of the profits to be made in the gold and mule trade. She then broadened her business interests to include these investments on the Chihuahua and Santa Fe Trails.

During these years Gertrudis Barceló became a woman of property, fame, and intrigue due largely to arriving American traders, and in particular, historian Josiah Gregg, who made his first trip to Santa Fe in 1831. Gregg described her as a woman "of loose habits."[44] According to journalist Matt Field of the New Orleans *Picayune,* Gertrudis also became known as a woman of influence among her peers, who "court her favor" while the "lowest look at her with wonder."[45] But the Department of New Mexico itself was gripped by Indian attacks and the misery they caused. New Mexicans believed that Governor Albino Pérez was responsible for the anguishing hunger and frostbitten fingers and toes of his militia. Although considered to be valorous, his brief tenure in office brought violent unrest in La Cañada de Santa Cruz in the Río Arriba, resulting in a rebellion that erupted in late 1837 led by governor-elect José Gonzales.

In the hopes of thwarting Gonzales, a *junta,* or tribunal, in Santa Fe was led by Vicente Sánchez Vergara. Food and loans were secured from foreign merchants to counter the hostile advance. *Ricos* from the Río Abajo contributed as much as 610 pesos apiece. Former Governor Manuel Armijo, an intimate friend of Tules, arrived in Santa Fe to quell the chaos.[46] The rampage gathered momentum as word passed from village to village.

Governor Pérez, a lover of extravagant furniture in the Palace of the Governors, favored a wardrobe trimmed with silver and beaver, and wore a gold watch worth three hundred pesos as he rode in an elaborate carriage drawn by a pair of fine horses costing eight hundred pesos. Added to his material extravagances was a mistress and housekeeper named Trinidad Trujillo, with whom he fathered a child.[47] Albino Pérez, considered an *estranjero,* or foreigner, to New Mexico, blatantly continued flaunting luxuries in the face of starvation and cold suffered by his militiamen. He raised taxes for education, an unpopular endeavor.

Gross neglect of northern New Mexico by the distant Mexican government following independence in 1821 led to the brutal assassination of Governor Pérez and sixteen of his officials—former governor Santiago Abréu and his two brothers, Ramon and Marcelino; Jesús María Alarid; Pablo Sáenz; Miguel Sena; Lieutenant José Hurtado; Alféreces Diego Sáenz, Juan Bustamente, and Juan López; Corporal Manuel Maldonado; Clarín Guadalupe Rodríguez; and militia soldiers Jaramillo, Ortega, José Loreto Escobar, and Manuel Madrid. Antonio Sena, neighbor and friend of Tules, was erroneously reported killed.[48]

These men had been killed with a savage vengeance. Governor Pérez was beheaded, his head mercilessly kicked around the Santa Fe plaza. An unparalleled footnote of heroism by the "Barceló women"—adopted daughters, friends, and no doubt the Doña herself leading the pack in 1837—is found in the notes of William G. Ritch, interim governor in 1875: "1837—Juana Prada, the Barcelonas and Pelegrina Domingues, the mother of Francisco Abreu, dressed in mens aparel visited the camp of the insurgents in the interest of Gov. Perez and discovered their desires refuted and besought Perez to leave. After Perez was killed the above women with Refugio Sisneros & Petra Gutierres, since the wife of JM Giddings still living, obtained the body and gave it burial."[49]

Amid the scene of political brutality in the streets of Santa Fe, daily life returned to normalcy—gambling.[50] In addition to gambling, the astute businesswoman known as La Tules participated in other ventures such as prostitution, mules, real estate, gold ventures, and trading. Josiah Gregg is remembered for his oft-repeated gossip about Doña Tules:

> She there became a constant attendant on one of those pande-
> moniums where the favorite game of monte was dealt *pro bono
> publico*. Fortune, at first, did not seem inclined to smile upon
> her efforts, and for some years she spent her days in lowliness
> and misery. At last her luck turned, as gamblers would say, and
> on one occasion she left the bank with a spoil of several hun-
> dred dollars! This enabled her to open a bank of her own, and
> being favored by a continuous run of good fortune, she gradu-
> ally rose higher and higher in the scale of affluence, until she
> found herself in possession of a very handsome fortune.[51]

To well-known New Mexicans, trail merchants, and writers of the time, the name of Doña Tules became familiar. They felt compelled to depict her as a woman "whose face . . . bore most unmistakably the impress of her fearful calling, being scarred and seamed, and rendered unwomanly by those painful lines which unbridled passions and midnight watching never fail to stamp upon the countenance of their votary."[52] Never in New Mexico's history has a woman attracted the attention of so many men, yet was simultaneously besmirched and ridiculed by them. In truth, they could not cope with her strong personality. At her death in 1852 a number of her critics still owed her money, from whom she instructed her executors to demand payment. Tules's business acumen reached well beyond the grave and into their pockets, the gamblers often leaving town as a result of her actions. She began to call in her debts via the courts.

In March 1848, Tules sued "James Hartly" [sic] and Henry Cuniffe, trading under the name of Hartly & Cuniffe. She had made them a loan a month earlier in the large amount of three thousand dollars at the monthly rate of 2 percent until paid.[53] Interest indeed gave Tules a comfortable income but made her extremely unpopular among those in her debt.

Doña Tules also sued George W. Coulter of the United States Hotel (also known as the Fonda and later the Exchange) for the five hundred dollars she had loaned him in 1848. August de Marle was sworn in before Judge Charles Beaubien on behalf of the plaintiff and testified regarding the arrangement negotiated in the world of gambling in early Santa Fe. The suit initially filed in Santa Fe County with the jury composed entirely of Anglos received a change of venue in April 1850 to Río Arriba County. The request was based on two reasons: "Because the public mind in this county is so prejudiced against the same that she cannot have a fair trial in the county of Santa Fe and that the friends of deft [defendant] in said cause have an undue influence in said county of Santa Fe so that a fair trial cannot be had in the same," signed by María Gertrudis Barceló.[54]

The Río Arriba proceedings, convened at Los Luceros north of today's Española, give a rare glimpse inside the nineteenth-century gambling world of the notorious gambling queen and her paramour, August de Marle. The basis of the suit was, of course, money. Coulter had borrowed $500 from Gertrudis Barceló, represented during the trial by the savvy de Marle. Coulter invited Tules to return to the hotel to deal her games; she judiciously refused to do so as long as Coulter owed her money. Coulter then made a proposal to de Marle and Tules whereby if they would return to the hotel to gamble he would pay her half of the amount owed ($250) and agree to accept the other half as table rent of $5 a night. Reluctantly, de Marle and Tules agreed to the proposal.

In December 1849, hotel proprietor George Coulter testified that he paid the pair $250 minus an amount for certain expenses. All went well for a brief time after the monte dealers returned to set up their games in the United States Hotel. After one day, however, a man or soldier by the name of More (Moore?) became violent due to the fact that Barceló and de Marle refused to loan him money. In a fit of temper Moore whipped out his gun and discharged a bullet toward the gamblers thus breaking up the game. The gallant Prussian de Marle shoved Tules under the monte table during the hostile encounter and shielded the shaken monte dealer with his body.[55] De Marle and Tules never returned to gamble at the hotel following the Moore episode. In an apparent effort to keep the peace in a highly charged atmosphere, the hotel proprietors (including a man named William Raymond) made bail for the rowdy gunman. The action by the hotel proprietors offended Tules. A final blow came when Coulter failed to make repayment of his debt to her in eight days as promised. Tules felt repeatedly deceived. In addition, she believed that Coulter kept a dangerous environment for her monte games. The shrewd monte dealer proved a tough opponent on and off the gambling table.

Violence in the United States Hotel occurred on a fairly regular basis it would seem. One stunned visitor to Santa Fe recalled in 1851: "A person came in, took a glass of brandy, turned from the bar and commenced firing his pistol at random, and could not be stopped until he had fired four shots which wounded one lawyer in the abdomen and another man in the arm. He was asked the reason for doing so and replied, 'A friend of his from Texas was killed at Santa Fe, and all inhabitants of the place were cutthroats, robbers and murderers.' He was a Texan. He was placed in jail. Later in the night, the Texan was taken from the jail and hung by the neck in the back yard of the Exchange. I suppose it was done by friends of the lawyer."[56]

In 1867 the most notable of shootings to occur in the hotel lobby

(now called the Exchange Hotel) was that of New Mexico's chief justice of the Territorial Supreme Court, John P. Slough, by attorney W. L.
Rynerson from southern Doña Ana County. Heated debates in the
post–Civil War atmosphere engendered violent rhetoric accompanied
by demands of public retraction. Rynerson appeared in the Exchange
with a Colt revolver concealed under a loose overcoat and after a quick
exchange of words pulled his weapon and fired a mortal wound into the
abdomen of Slough.[57]

Later, the bloody history of the Exchange Hotel included the scandalous shooting in 1879 of the French architect François Mallet, who
was working on the St. Francis Cathedral, by a nephew and namesake of
Archbishop Jean Baptiste Lamy. Mallet was seen in the hotel apparently
having an affair with the wealthy Mercedes Chaves, daughter of former
governor José Chaves of Los Padillas, New Mexico.

Back to the Barceló-Coulter trial. From 1847 to 1850, Doña Tules
pursued the debt of G. W. Coulter of the United States Hotel with dogged
determination. After the first, all-Anglo jury failed to reach an agreement on damages and was discharged, the Los Luceros jury rendered a
verdict that Coulter had to pay Tules $257 of the original $500 debt.[58]

This lawsuit stamps an indelible pro-American predilection on the
monte dealer like no other historical document found. It also illustrates
the prejudice, whether by "sore losers" from the gaming table or the general public in Santa Fe, against Tules at the time.

CHAPTER FOUR

Los Americanos

~⟩

By January 1846, duties on wagonloads from Missouri to Santa Fe amounted to five hundred dollars a wagon. The tariff, which was considerably less than the stiff eighteen hundred to twenty-five hundred dollars per wagon load theoretically required by Mexican law, failed to paralyze trade on the Santa Fe Trail. Within three months Manuel Armijo, described by U.S. consul Manuel Alvarez as "a good man in small matters . . . a small one in great affairs," had assumed his duties for a short-lived third term as governor of New Mexico.[1] The American traders were looking forward to more favorable treatment and many more festive bailes or fandangos in the Palace of the Governors.

On March 6, 1846, the traders in Santa Fe gave an elaborate ball for Armijo the same day he assumed office. A bedecked and rotund Governor Armijo appeared in his blue frocked coat with rolled collar, a general's shoulder straps, blue striped trousers trimmed with gold lace, and a dapper red sash around his body. He boldly proclaimed that "if war were declared there would be no fighting by the people of New

FIGURE 6. ✌ Manuel Armijo (ca. 1793–1853), general and Mexican governor
of New Mexico. (From drawing in pastel and charcoal, ca.
1845). Museum of New Mexico neg. no. 50809.

Mexico."[2] Armijo boasted as well, "Dios en el cielo y Armijo en la tierra"
(God rules the heavens and Armijo rules the earth). All looked rosy
indeed until the political climate quickly changed. Armijo ordered all
Americans in the Taos vicinity to return to the interior of New Mexico
for their safety. War loomed on the horizon—the U.S.–Mexican War.
    American soldiers under General Stephen Watts Kearny marched

into New Mexico in mid-August 1846 and met with no resistance at Apache Canyon, approximately twenty miles southeast of Santa Fe. In the midst of chaos with his troops lacking training and supplies, Governor Armijo abandoned the fight before it ever began. With a number of companions, one being his secretary Antonio Sena, Doña Tules's neighbor and confidante, Armijo fled south to Chihuahua, a distance of more than five hundred miles. Armijo's haste was so great that in Santa Fe he abandoned his state coach, a gilded and lumbering affair unsuitable for a swift retreat across rugged terrain. He also abandoned his corpulent wife, who retreated to Albuquerque.[3]

The New Mexico family of Gertrudis Barceló today believes that the fleeing Mexican governor was given temporary refuge east of Albuquerque in the Manzano home of María de la Luz Barceló, Tules's younger sister.[4] Armijo, known monte partner and paramour of Doña Tules, had lived up to his word of no military resistance, steadfastly refusing to become a dead hero.[5] A bitter contemporary wrote that he was "no paragon of bravery, virtue, or honesty."[6] Another rumor circulated that Antonio Sena claimed the governor had accepted five hundred ounces of gold from Captain Philip St. George Cooke to lead no resistance against the Americans.[7] New Mexico was a spider web of unfounded rumors in 1846.

Governor Armijo traveled down El Camino Real to Mexico City, where he stayed until the spring of 1847, facing charges of treason and cowardice. Eventually cleared of the charges, Armijo returned to New Mexico a disillusioned man and a persona non grata. He died in 1854 in the southern village of Lemitar and was buried in the church wall at nearby Socorro, New Mexico.[8]

An 1846 edition of the *Niles' National Register* recorded the so-called bloodless arrival of the Americans in Santa Fe:

The head of the column arrived in sight of the town about three:—it was six before the van came up. [Donaciano] Vigil, the lieutenant governor, and twenty or thirty of the people of the town, received us at the Palace. The general [Kearny] addressed them in a speech little different in substance, but much in manner, which was conversational, as at the Vegas and San Miguel. We were then asked to partake of wine and brandy, of domestic manufacture, it was from the Passo del Norte [El Paso].[9] We were too thirsty to judge of its merits. Anything liquid and cool was palatable. During the repast, and as the sun was setting, the United States flag was hoisted on the palace, and a salute of 13 guns fired from the artillery that was left on an eminence overlooking the town [later site of Fort Marcy].

The ceremony ended; the general and his staff were invited to supper at Capt. Hortises [Ortíz's], a Mexican gentleman, once in the army. The supper was served very much after the manner of a French dinner, one dish succeeding another, in endless succession. A bottle of good wine from the Passo del Norte, and a loaf of bread were placed near each plate. We had been from five in the morning without eating, and endless as were the dishes, more endless still were our appetites.

We returned to the palace, where we found Mr. [Lucius] Thruston, an American, with an invitation to another supper, at the celebrated Madame Tula's. This is a lady who has amassed a large fortune here and at Chihuahua, by gambling and other accomplishments. A few of us went down [to Burro Alley]. We found the lady a little *passee*, but by far the most vivacious and intelligent Mexican we had yet seen. I wished to make observations; and, after gratifying my curiosity by a survey of her spacious and well furnished halls, I returned to my quarters, where I found my people all so much fagged, that I determined to follow their example and go to bed.[10]

Other accounts tell of the social events of August 1846. Expenses for a boisterous ball hosting the people of Santa Fe at the United States Hotel by General Kearny, the statement signed by him, totaled $166.17.[11] The bill for a lively "fandango," as it was called, listed a glass-breakage allowance, as well as an amount for the repair of the ballroom. Liquors, wine, and brandy of El Paso topped the expenses at $48.50. There were musicians ($11.50) and playing cards ($4.50), the latter indicating that there was, of course, gambling.[12] Tules, the reigning queen of monte, wisely reserved her graceful presence for a more intimate affair in her own famous sala. Her attendance guaranteed any successful Santa Fe soirée.

In 1846 Chihuahua trader and Spanish-speaking American Lucius

Thruston, a friend of Doña Tules for possibly twenty years, graciously invited the American military to her Burro Alley sala for a late night dinner.[13] Significantly, this would be the first encounter by the woman gambler with American soldiers and officers, who became some of her most select patrons at the monte table. Eleven years earlier in 1835 the hospitable Thruston had been the center of a dispute with Ana María Rendón, a neighbor of Doña Tules. She appeared before the alcalde or magistrate complaining that the Doña was illegally cohabiting with Thruston.[14] Confronted by Tules, Ana María recanted her charge, saying that she meant only that she [Tules] was "living in the same house." Other unspecified slander arose in the alcalde court that year from Josefa Tenorio.[15] As Doña Tules gained power and wealth during her climb to fame, envy inevitably followed.

Arriving with the American occupation were Susan Magoffin and her new husband Samuel, both from Kentucky, who met and entertained prominent people of the era, including Lucius Thruston.[16] Susan wrote: "Mr. T. [Thruston] is a friend of Gen. Kearny's and I believe about to receive an office from him; he is a gentleman I should judge who had seen a good deal of the world, is easy and familiar in his manners. As he leaves with the Gen. day after tomorrow, he will be happy to call on me on his return two weeks hence, and learn something of his old friends in Ky."[17]

Lucius Thruston and other Americans lived in the adobe house of Doña Tules. An entrepreneur involved in many different endeavors, including that of landlady, Tules by 1851 rented rooms in her home to Major John Munroe, the civil and military governor of New Mexico, and Lieutenant Lafayette McLaws of the U.S. Army. An official document shows the government spent a total amount of $645 per month for several rentals in Santa Fe.[18] Once the Americans arrived in New Mexico, the prices of food and housing had increased dramatically. The population of Santa Fe increased as well.

If Doña Tules was indeed running a house of prostitution in the mid-1830s or living as a *barragana*, or concubine, to Governor Manuel Armijo, only limited information may be drawn from the Ana María Rendón charges or certain other sources. Nevertheless, rumors persisted concerning her role as a madam in the many hearsay accounts written from Santa Fe by tourists and traders. The rather astonished war correspondent Richard Smith Elliott claimed that during her prime, Tules had "a score of lovers at a time."[19] Then in a more charitable tone he added, "Though a little *passe*, she had been, in youth, very beautiful and very much admired—*and*, it is said, so full of warmth was her woman's heart in years gone by, that it animated in her breast the most lively emotions."[20] In other words, Tules was truly a charismatic and passionate woman. Historians have discovered no photograph or daguerreotype of her as yet, however. Would she even be recognized as Gertrudis Barceló?

The hypothesis by some historians that prostitution, though seldom discussed in early documents, did not thrive in New Mexico until the arrival of the American army is debatable. Organized prostitution as a profession indeed may have arrived with the Army of the West and with it venereal disease, which increased with the American occupation. Regarding prostitutes, the U.S. census of 1850 lists a number of "courtesans," with the youngest given as eleven years old in Las Vegas, New Mexico.[21]

While in Santa Fe in 1846, trader Samuel Magoffin and his wife Susan attended lively fandangos. They observed the New Mexican women smoking their cigarillos and dancing the *cuna* (meaning cradle)— including the "old woman with false hair and teeth (doña Tula) . . . a stately dame of a certain age, the possessor of a portion of that shrewd sense and fascinating manner necessary to allure the wayward, inexperienced youth to the hall of final ruin."[22] The account by Susan Magoffin gives a rare feminine portrayal of Tules, the ambitious gambler behind the stacks of gold coins.

Hard specie was nonexistent in Santa Fe during the fall of 1846. There was no money with which to pay the U.S. troops. Nor was there money to clothe, equip, and feed the one hundred elite Chihuahua Rangers under Lieutenant Colonel David Dawson Mitchell's command. The rangers were about to march to Chihuahua to engage in battle against the Mexican soldiers.[23] General Kearny earlier alerted the chief paymaster of the Army of the West that as much gold as possible would be needed to pay the troops; this was supplemented with treasury drafts, which ultimately proved worthless. Chief Paymaster Robert Walker brought twenty thousand dollars in gold, drafts, some small bank notes of the Bank of Missouri, and small coins. Within four months following

FIGURE 7. ❧ David Dawson Mitchell (1806–61). Courtesy of Charles Mitchell.

the army's arrival U.S. paymaster Captain William S. Murphy was dead broke—that is, until he returned on the Santa Fe Trail in January 1847 with $120,000.[24]

Interestingly, the U.S.–Mexican War became the first war in which the quartermaster department was totally responsible for the procurement, storage, and distribution of clothing to the army.[25] As for hard specie, the one opportunistic civilian dealing in large sums of money was gambler Doña Tules. Correspondent Richard Smith Elliott wrote an embellished version of a loan *negocio* by the erudite and handsome Colonel Mitchell.[26] The colonel desperately needed a thousand dollars for a worthy cause, his Chihuahua-bound troops.

The six-foot-six-inch Lucius Thruston, who was forced to stoop to enter the low doorways of New Mexico houses, again enters the picture. Lieutenant R. S. Elliott, perhaps referring to Thruston's height, wrote: "A gentleman of Santa Fe *who stands high* [author's italics] in the Doña's estimation—an American of long residence, who speaks the Spanish language well—was invited to the Colonel's quarters next day, and the subject [of a loan] broached to him."[27] The following day, paymasters, colonels, majors, and adjutants converged at the residence of Doña Tules, according to Elliott. Elegant pier-glass mirrors decorated the mud walls, while Brussels rugs covered the mud floors.[28] As the soldiers lounged on *bancos* of rolled blankets against the wall and sipped chocolate, *la señora* rolled cigarritos from cornhusks and tobacco for her guests. The delicate issue of a loan serendipitously arose. Acting as interpreter, Thruston drew on his eloquent Mexican diplomacy to approach the reluctant Doña Tules. The expedition of ninety-five rather than one hundred Chihuahua Rangers hung in the balance.

The next day an orderly from Colonel Mitchell with a gilt-edged letter carefully tied with pink and blue ribbons arrived at the Doña's door to entice her into granting the loan. Such attentiveness wooed the lady. At the appointed time, Mitchell in full uniform accompanied Doña Tules, elegantly dressed in silk and jewelry, on his arm to the play *Pizarro* in the Palace of Governors, performed by the army volunteers.[29] After the play and social, Mitchell escorted Tules to her door late that evening. According to correspondent Elliott, "a good night such as angels might smile upon was exchanged."[30]

The elite Chihuahua Rangers soon departed, the suave Colonel Mitchell giving Tules a cavalier bow from his favorite gray mount, "a chilly acknowledgment" of her generosity.[31] William Clark Kennerly related that a war correspondent in Santa Fe, no doubt Richard Smith Elliott, attempted to send an account of the affair to his St. Louis paper. Colonel Mitchell threatened to shoot him if he succeeded.[32]

In 1846 a summer of some discontent reigned in Santa Fe. Chihuahua trader William Henry Glasgow expressed his utter disgust, saying that Mitchell "never failed from the first day he entered this place to importune and harrass Co¹ Doniphan to leave the place and not allow the interest of a *few paltry speculators* [the trail merchants] to influence his movements." Mitchell obtained "a universal contempt for him as an officer & a most cordial hatred as a man," according to Glasgow.[33]

The question arises whether the U.S. army repaid the thousand-dollar loan or if Colonel Mitchell indeed used the money for the historically touted purpose, that of supplies and clothing for his men.[34] David Dawson Mitchell proved to be a worldly man. In 1833 he was acting bourgeois of the American Fur Company at Fort Union on the Upper Missouri River before becoming an Indian agent in St. Louis. He accompanied Maximilian, prince of Wied, and artist Karl Bodmer up the Missouri River by keelboat in 1833 from Fort Union to Fort McKenzie.[35] The cultivated Mitchell married two or more Indian women according to their traditions, siring Assiniboine and Sac and Fox children.[36] But unquestionably, Mitchell would never have left his beloved Martha Eliza, the city wife whom he had married in 1840. For that matter, nor would the seasoned traveler have left St. Louis to travel the eight hundred miles to Santa Fe without adequate funds to provide for unforeseen contingencies.[37]

With his personal funds, it appears that D. D. Mitchell and other members of the military might have been some of the earliest American speculators in New Mexico land in 1846. A deed dated December 20, 1846, deemed a spurious document by Judge William Blackmore, was discovered in 1890s.[38] The deed indicated that Charles Beaubien and wife Paula, Charles Bent, Guadalupe Miranda, and Mexican governor Manuel Armijo sold five-sixths of the Río de las Animas Grant to Lieutenant Colonel David D. Mitchell, Major Benjamin Walker, Dunham Spaulding, Captain Thomas Hudson, and New Mexico chief justice Joab Houghton.[39]

Following the departure of Colonel Mitchell and his Chihuahua Rangers from Santa Fe in December 1846, an insurgency in the form of a conspiracy, involving men from the Taos area, soon erupted. A plan for a Christmas Eve revolt against American control was temporarily foiled until early 1847. Artist Alfred S. Waugh, known for his sketch of

Governor Armijo, aptly described the spy network of Doña Tules: "To this Señora, the Governor communicates all the affairs of the State, she then gives them to her adopted daughter [Petra Gutierres], who is married to an American resident [James M. Giddings], and from whom the daughter they go to her husband, thus they go from one to another until every movement becomes known to our people in the capital." One account alleges that a mulatto girl who was married to one of the conspirators leaked the information to Colonel Price.[40] Through this feminine grapevine, the Barceló women kept the Americans apprised of a potential uprising, and one ultimately occurred.

The "Barceló women," as they were called, may have included various other prostitutes. It is through jealous innuendo that we learn more about Madam Tules and her retinue of girls. The five-foot-two-inch-tall Spaniard, Manuel Alvarez, claiming then disclaiming Spanish, Mexican, and U.S. citizenship while in contradiction serving as U.S. consul in Santa Fe, scribbled the following thoughts on the reverse of an unrelated letter. The consul continued to jot barbed notes in 1847 regarding Doña Tules and her influence over the American officers. Alvarez, who later witnessed Tules's will in 1850, made the following comments:

> [April 1847]
> Though Mr. Price cannot dispose of any troops of his command for any useful purpose of this county the 27th of this month he has through galantry *or otherwise* [author's italics] granted a detachment of troops as escort under command of one officer to the celebrated Mme. Tules that Mr. [George W.] Kendall of the Picayune [New Orleans newspaper] notices in his book as a French modiste.[41] Though Mr. Kendall has mistakened her nationality since she is of the purest blood of the Montes and that I doubt much that she ever made a stitche with the needle he is very right in what he says in relation to her helping, particularly the young merchants in disposing of their silks, satins, calicoes, etc., in this line of business she never had her like equal here. . . . God knows which of her immense talents she made use for to acquire her influence upon Mr. [Sterling] Price, but the fact is that she has obtain[ed] what the Governor and the other most respectable citizens could not obtain of him, and what she

never could obtain of the most profligate of the late Mexican commanders.[42]

Manuel Alvarez proved correct in his account of the military escort for Doña Tules. Returning twelve days later on May 7, 1847, the American soldiers who accompanied Tules to Manzano and other places south included Second Lieutenant August de Marle (a new lover) and four privates, members of Company B, Battalion Missouri Light Artillery, Missouri Volunteers. All were Prussians from St. Louis, who made exceptionally well-disciplined soldiers.[43]

Santa Fe never lacked for entertainment after the arrival of the Americans. In December 1847, a year following the opening of the U.S.–Mexican War, a ball was given at the United States Hotel in honor of captains William Z. Angney and Cerán St. Vrain, heroes of the bloody Taos rebellion.[44] The *Santa Fe Republican* described the array of women with lustrous eyes, smiles, silks, satins, flounces and furbelows. "Madame T [Tules] was there, as young and blooming as we ever saw her, and seemed to enjoy it."[45] Two weeks later, General Kearny gave a large ball to honor Colonel Sterling Price. Again, the *Republican* lavished its verbose prose, stressing the sobriety and respectfulness of the affair—"Black eyes, all sorts of eyes were there. Busts, women a Phadeus [Pheidias, Greek sculptor] might take for a model, but what we admired most was the fine forms, the graceful carriage, and the ease and dignity of the fair."[46] The social life in Santa Fe surely required enormous stamina by the gambler called La Tules, who, after dancing away the evening, played monte the remainder of the night.

Extravagant galas continued in Santa Fe—yet another was given by the American son-in-law of Doña Tules: "Those that had the privilege and we pity those who had not of attending the soirée on Monday evening, given by James Giddings, in honor of the return of General [*sic*] Price, witnessed something of the kind unequaled as yet in Santa Fe. It is needless to expatiate on the beauty of the fair guests, the splendor of the decorations, and the courtesy of M.G. [Mr. Giddings?]—suffice it to say, every [blank] was 'comme il fait.'"[47]

Business as usual continued between parties in Santa Fe. Large wagons continued to ply the Chihuahua and Santa Fe Trails as they had done several years earlier in 1840 when Trinidad Barceló, brother of Doña Tules, received two *guías*, or commercial passports, required for freighting between Mexican provinces: one dated August 11, 1840, for 100 *bultos* of domestic merchandise with a value of 815 pesos, destined for Sonora, and *fiador*, or guarantor, Dolores Madrid; and the other dated August 14, 1840, for 46 bultos valued at 348 pesos 1 real, destined also for Sonora, fiador Francisco Ortíz y Delgado.[48] Another guía dated October 10, 1845, for "foreign merchandise," valued at 106 pesos 20 cents, was destined for El Paso. Categories were bultos, *tercios, cajones*, bailes, and *piezas*. Various terms described the way the goods were packed, rather than volume, weight, or value. It should be noted that an Antonio Moreno, part of the Sonoran Barceló family, also received a guía on August 3, 1840, the same date as Trinidad Barceló, for 18 bultos of domestic merchandise valued at 222 pesos 4 reales, destined for Sonora.[49]

Love, monte, and intrigue occupied the notorious life of Gertrudis Barceló. The sporting society of Santa Fe also enjoyed horse racing, but not without its fixing. In 1839 Manuel Chaves, a relative by marriage to Doña Tules, instigated a horse race that he thought would ensure an easy win for Tules. Unfortunately, Manuel Armijo conspired with the French doctor Philippe Auguste Masure to poison Chaves's favored horse on which Tules had bet but which mysteriously dropped dead before reaching the finish line. The smug Armijo had covered all bets and reaped the large proceeds. Whereupon, the embittered Manuel Chaves planned an assassination plot against Armijo as the governor left the Palace of Governors to visit Tules's nearby sala. The attempt failed and Chaves left town on the Santa Fe Trail.[50]

Prussian August de Marle of the Missouri Volunteers in 1846 wrote to his St. Louis German friends that the soldiers had built a superb fort [Marcy] in order to protect Santa Fe. He acquired a passion for the Spanish language, which he considered "the noblest, clearest and richest" of all the languages he had studied. He discovered New Mexico women to be emancipated, whereupon when he entered a room he heard whispers of "mi alma, mi curacion [*corazón*, heart], mi querido [dear]." His personal opinion expressed "that this land [New Mexico] will never remain a part of the United States." He continued, "The language and the religion constitute a people; all other boundaries are a makeshift, the work of map-makers." De Marle ceased writing articles to the St. Louis German newspaper. As the new lover of Doña Tules he was busily "paying court to the richest, most interesting, and most esteemed widow in New Mexico."[51]

Many Americans remained in Santa Fe after 1846 and married daughters of New Mexico. Their descendants live there today. Although the Hispanic culture forever changed after the U.S.–Mexican War, many centuries-old traditions survived the American influence thrust on them. The traditions are celebrated today with enthusiasm, though perhaps lacking some of the lost historical knowledge behind them. Women like the legendary Doña Gertrudis Barceló remain a part of New Mexico history, only to become more legendary over time.

CHAPTER 5

"The Hall of Final Ruin" and Other Real Estate

⤳

L egend recounts that the gambling sala of Doña Tules, termed "the hall of final ruin" by the young Kentucky bride Susan Magoffin, was located on Burro Alley. Perhaps that was true in August 1846. Nevertheless, during her twenty-year career Doña Tules apparently dealt monte in several other places in Santa Fe—on the south side of the plaza near the Giddings-Gentry store, on the east side of the plaza in the space later occupied by the barbershop of African American George Carter in the 1870s, and at the southeast corner of the plaza in the United States Hotel, today's La Fonda.[1]

St. Louis war correspondent Richard Smith Elliott wrote some of the most accurate information known about Doña Tules in April 1847.[2] He criticized Matt Field (known as Phazma), a journalist for the *New Orleans Picayune* and the *St. Louis Reveille*, and Josiah Gregg in his *Commerce of the Prairies* for their inaccuracies, claiming Tules's heritage to be French and confusing her with her sister-in-law Dolores Barceló who gambled in Taos.

FIGURE 8. ⊰ Exchange Hotel (La Fonda) and Southeast Corner of Plaza, Santa Fe, New Mexico, ca. 1855. Museum of New Mexico neg. no. 10685.

Richard Elliott placed Doña Tules in a "tavern" located on the plaza. He wrote: "Here we are at the door. It is the bar-room, well-supplied with liquors and other refreshments, to wit: *pies*. . . . We enter—now we turn through a door to the right, and . . . are almost suffocated by the dust arising from the earthen floor. It is a small room, and there, behind a table, sits Tules, now in the act of throwing out the cards to determine the bets amounting to perhaps two hundred dollars."[3]

Eight years earlier in 1839, however, journalist Matt Field had described a large room, the dimensions corresponding to those of the Barceló property at the southeast corner of Palace Avenue at Burro Alley. He wrote: "The apartment in which we were received was about fifty feet in length by twenty in width, one end of it completely carpeted. . . . her bank was open almost every evening, (not in her own house but in another part of the city)."[4] This might indicate that the Burro Alley gambling sala was yet to be opened by 1839.[5]

Soon after the arrival of the Americans in August 1846 the popular

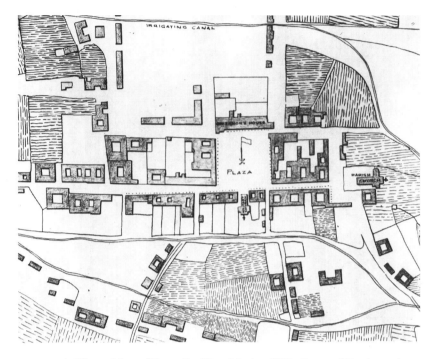

MAP 1. ❧ Gilmer Map of Santa Fe, New Mexico (U.S. Corps of Engineers),
ca. 1846. Museum of New Mexico neg. no. 111078.

Fonda became known as the United States Hotel. And until Doña Tules
acquired the four buildings at the convergence of today's Palace Avenue,
Burro Alley, and Grant Avenue, she appeared to be moving around in
the vicinity of Santa Fe's plaza, choosing the lucrative and "shady pre-
cincts of the hotels."[6] It was in the United States Hotel (La Fonda) on the
southeast corner of the plaza that she and her companion, the Prussian
dealer August de Marle, survived a shooting episode by hiding under a
monte table, the encounter discussed in an earlier chapter.[7]

In 1848 traveler George Douglass Brewerton narrated that he was
escorted into a villainous-smelling bar before entering a second apartment which was the principal gambling saloon of Santa Fe. He depicted
a "long, low room, with narrow windows upon one side, which lighted
it but dimly, and an earthen floor, which seemed perfectly impregnated
with the expectorations of its tobacco-chewing frequenters." Brewerton
continued, "On either side of this apartment were ranged three tables

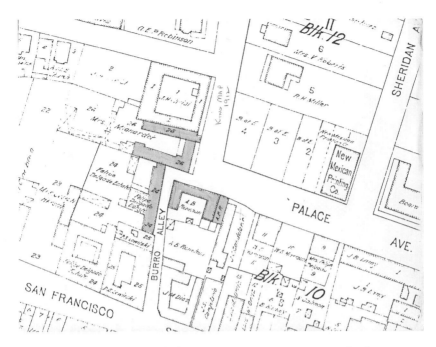

MAP 2. ❧ King's Map detail of Santa Fe, New Mexico, 1912. Author's
collection.

for the convenience of the 'banks' and their customers . . . the tables
strongly built with a wooden parapet upon the three sides most distant
from the wall . . . to stop any undesirable scrutiny into the manipula-
tions of the banker."[8] The Santa Fe visitor later encountered his Missouri
guide seated on the driver's box of his mule wagon bound for Chihuahua,
ranting about his loss of money "thanks to that cussed *Monté* woman,
flat broke."[9]

   Omissions bedevil early Santa Fe deed records of the Spanish and
Mexican periods. In piecing together various travelers' accounts with
descriptions found in adjoining real estate deeds and in the bequests of
the Doña's last will and testament, an intriguing picture of her land ownership emerges. Just as compelling are the hypothetical motives behind
their acquisition. For example, by owning the four adjacent properties
at the west end of today's Palace Avenue at its convergence with Burro
Alley, including that of her residence which faced directly into Palace

FIGURE 9. ❧ Residence of Doña Tules, intersection of Burro Alley,
            Palace, and Grant avenues, Santa Fe, New Mexico, ca. 1910.
            Museum of New Mexico neg. no. 11284.

FIGURE 10. ❧ Detail of residence of Doña Tules, facing Grant Avenue, Santa
            Fe, New Mexico. Museum of New Mexico neg. no. 94625.

Avenue at Grant Avenue, she established what might be termed a security zone. Thus the Doña and her associates could move freely from building to building without unnecessary or dangerous exposure to potential crime. Remember, there were neither banks nor policemen at the time, and Tules and her *compadres* were moving heavy bags of gold dust and coins.[10]

The lower Palace Avenue area, facing the Calle de la Muralla (muralla, the old presidio wall) and in 1841 designated as part of the Barrio Torreón, was an ideal location for gambling and prostitution.[11] One great advantage was its accessibility to and uninterrupted view of the Palace of the Governors. The location gave ready access to the bulging pockets of trappers and traders fresh off the Chihuahua and Santa Fe Trails. Trail-weary freighters quickly visited the dram shops (saloons) and gaming tables throughout Santa Fe, often losing a year's profit. In 1846 American officers and poorly equipped soldiers, who willingly and quite literally bet their bottom dollar down to their uniform buttons and infrequently washed socks, patronized Tules's gambling sala to the point of dissipation.[12]

Some of the adobe buildings once owned by Doña Tules at the Burro Alley intersection survived well into the twentieth-century lifetime of this writer, though they have since been demolished.[13] On August 6, 1844, Gertrudis Barceló requested a formalization of title to her house and land.[14] This was her house and residence facing eastward toward the plaza. The legal instrument is the earliest deed of record regarding her Santa Fe property ownership. Found in the title petition, a part of the property was first conveyed to her by Francisco Baca y Ortíz, who witnessed her will in 1850, and another part by District Court Judge Santiago Abréu, whose bloody assassination by dismemberment had occurred seven years earlier during the Río Arriba uprising of 1837.[15] The formalization of title request reads as follows:

> In the City of Santa Fe, Capital of the Department of New Mexico on the sixth day of the month of August, current year of one thousand eight hundred and forty-four: Before me, the Citizen Tomas Ortiz, 1st Constitutional Alcalde of this illustrious Ayuntamiento or municipal government, and before my ordinary, assistant witness with whom I act as Actuary or

FIGURE 11. ⊱ Intersection of Burro Alley, Palace, and Grant avenues,
Santa Fe, New Mexico, ca. 1931. Right, Barceló residence
and, left, site of gambling sala. Museum of New Mexico
neg. no 132163.

FIGURE 12. ⊱ Burro Alley, Santa Fe, New Mexico, looking north toward
Barceló residence, ca. 1899–1905. Photo by C. G. Kaadt.
Museum of New Mexico neg. no. 11070.

Delegate Judge, for lack of a public notary that there is none, and these serving as proof will be named at the end, appeared present in her proper person Doña Maria Gertrudis Barceló, whom I declare to know, and stated that as the house used for her residence, has not the proper title that must show the property that she has in it. I will condescend to make or draw up one to which she is entitled to; in virtue of which I, the present Judge proceed to form the present document in favor of the Lady [Sra.], which asks about the mentioned house, which is composed of nine rooms, another house for habitation or abode, with its "placita" or small square and porches in the center, a "zaguan" or hall, and its front a porch toward the South; it must be observed that five rooms of the mentioned house to the eastern side were bought from Don Francisco Baca y Ortiz, and he was present and he acknowledged before me that it was true, and the other rooms were built by same "Sra." Or Lady in land that she bought from the deceased Santiago Abreu, and there was present and appeared before me his widow, the wife of the deceased, Doña Josefa Baca and she assures that it is true.

To this house there is joined a piece of land on the western side, which land was bought from Pablito Ortiz (now deceased) and his son D. Juan being present stated that it was true, this land is bounded on the North with the fence which divides the land of Sr. Juan Rafael Esquibel; on the South, by lands of Don Blas Roibal; on the East, by the same house of the Sra. or Lady; on the West with the fence which divides the land of Don Anastacio Sandoval. And because Doña Gertrudes Barcelo having established that she is the only owner of the prementioned house and land; I confer on her the most forceful and effective title and document for her security. And the boundaries of the house are: On the North, by the mentioned Juan Rafael Esquibel; on the South, the Street and another house belonging to the same Sra. or Lady; on the East, the Street looking this way; on the West, by lands of the same owner; which property she declares not having sold or alienated, and that the property is free of any tribute, testament, Capeliana viriculo patronato bond or any other obligation, perpetual or royal, temporary, special, general, tacit or implied, or expressed, and so I formed and executed this document, with all entrances and exits, center, part of building which projects beyond the wall only, customs, convenience, rights and any other causes or bonds which they might have had, and which might belong to them according to law, so that for herself her heirs, and successors may enjoy it, may exchange, alienate, and dispose of same in favor of any one they may elect, as a matter belonging to them adjudicated with legitimate and just title. And I empower her irrevocably with free and privilege and general administration, and I constitute them, as attorneys and plaintiffs in their own cause, so that they may stay and possess the mentioned house and lands.—So that she will acquire the judicial and royal holding and possession, and by virtue of this document, no one shall bring suit against the Sra. or lady, nor her children, nor make any demand whatsoever, on this property. And as Competent Judge I give title in her favor, found on the right of possession that the Sra. or Lady has acquired, purchases that I give her credit for having done in the mentioned manner; To all of which I sanction, approve and confirm by the authority of the law vested in me, being instrumental witnesses the C.C. Cap'n. Don Anto. Sena, D. Santiago Armijo, and D. Benito Larragoitia who were present and residents of this City. I so certify.[16]

Tomas Ortiz (rubric)

Using the vague description common for the time in 1844, the Gertrudis Barceló house, where the Santa Fe County Courthouse stands today, might have resembled the floor-plan sketch dictated by two of the families who lived in it.[17] Each complained of awakening to intruders digging in the placita, presumably for the buried gold of Doña Tules. Although the configuration of the many rooms suggests a suitable arrangement for a bordello, it has not been found described as such in early documents.

Ten months following Gertrudis Barceló's death in early 1852 a brief notice appeared in the *Santa Fe Weekly Gazette* stating that its office had moved into the house "formerly occupied by the late Gertrude Barcelo."[18] The newspaper's masthead touted an editorial policy of "Independent

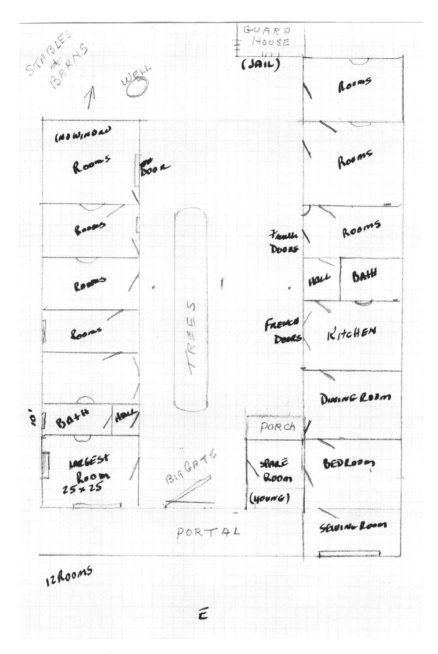

DRAWING 1. ✢ Floor plan of residence of Doña Tules. Sketch by Tony
Mignardot. Author's collection.

in all things—Neutral in nothing," an apt epitaph for the former well-known houseowner as well.[19]

The chain of title of this property records a who's who of nineteenth-century New Mexico history. It reveals that following her death the residence of Doña Tules, described in one deed as "where she lived and died," was sold in December 1854 for one thousand dollars by her sister María de la Luz Barceló to James L. Collins, adjoining neighbor and gambler friend of Tules. Five months later in May 1855 Collins conveyed it with "natural love and affection" to his daughter, Eliza Ann Edgar, then a resident of Boonville, Cooper County, Missouri.[20]

Born around 1801 at Crab Orchard, Kentucky, the red-haired Squire Collins was called a blackleg, or professional gambler, and "his worst personal enemy" by Acting Governor W. W. H. Davis. Collins, who moved from Kentucky to Missouri, arrived in New Mexico around 1826, where he traded until 1846.[21] On his *carta de seguridad*, or safe-conduct pass, to travel within the Mexican republic he stated that he was a justice of the peace at Franklin, Missouri, a merchant in Chihuahua by 1830, and by 1846 the chief interpreter for Colonel Alexander Doniphan during the U.S.–Mexican War. James L. Collins was principal owner and editor of the *Santa Fe Weekly Gazette* in the 1850s, superintendent of Indian affairs in New Mexico from 1857 to 1863, and later in charge of the government depository in Santa Fe. In 1867 Collins was elected as one of the first trustees of the Presbyterian Church in Santa Fe. The colorful Colonel Collins was found shot to death in the depository, the result of a bungled burglary or self-inflicted bullet.[22]

The *Weekly Gazette* recorded the numerous improvements in Santa Fe, commenting in 1858 that "in every direction there seems to be preparation for building of some kind." James Collins "is regenerating" his property "radically" and laying the foundation for a future building project.[23] Collins had also purchased adjacent property to the north of his own house in 1853. The Indian agency was later located there.[24]

For the sum of five thousand dollars in 1865 James M. and Eliza Ann Edgar conveyed the Barceló residence to Genoveva Archuleta de Ruhe, the mother and guardian of Carlota de los Dolores Ruhe.[25] New Mexico territorial secretary William G. Ritch acquired the mortgage deed in 1886. Thereafter, the residence of Doña Tules became known as the Ritch property.[26] Former secretary Ritch added a new cornice to the adobe house and made other improvements in 1886, which perhaps included the brick coping typical of territorial in style.[27] W. G. Ritch assigned the mortgage, with unpaid principal, interest, and taxes amounting to seven thousand dollars, to Judge Samuel B. Axtell in 1886.[28]

From Axtell the property then passed in 1907 to a minor, Henry W. Phillips. That same year Celina Mignardot acquired the Barceló residence.[29] By 1928 Jay L. Young, who sold Singer Sewing Machines, leased the house, enclosed a small front room called the "sewing room" by the Mignardots, and opened a real estate office.[30] The historic adobe house once belonging to the famous Doña Tules was demolished in 1939 when the Santa Fe County Courthouse was constructed.[31]

Diagonally from the above Barceló residence on the southeast corner of Palace Avenue at Burro Alley was once the gambling sala of the Doña.[32] In her will Doña Tules bequeathed this house and property to Rallitos (Rayos) Gutierres, her favorite adopted granddaughter. Dolores Barceló (wife of Trinidad) occupied this house in 1850. James M. Giddings with his wife, the mother of Rallitos, lived in an adjoining house to the east, which apparently shared the same lot. Following the marriage of Rallitos to Indian agent Lorenzo Labadie, the Burro Alley-Palace Avenue corner was sold to Felix and Cleofas García in 1854 for three hundred dollars. Nine years later it was deeded for four hundred dollars to John T. Russell and James L. Collins. After being owned by William H. Manderfield, guardian of Sallie Russell, daughter of John, the property was deeded to Charles H. and Teresita M. Gildersleeve, who in turn sold it in April 1902 to William H. and Florence E. Bartlett. In December 1903 Zepora Gold and Alois B. Renehan became owners.[33] The original building may have been demolished in 1904 for the new Renehan "mission style" residence, described by the local newspaper as the most modern in Santa Fe.[34]

Over the years the Renehan building housed the charming Mariposa Shop, which sold arts and crafts, run by Olive Wilson L'Amoreux, then a Museum of New Mexico librarian.[35] The shop closed in 1926 with a farewell tea lamenting the fate of historic Burro Alley. Fear for the preservation of the ancient alley ran through the streets of old Santa Fe when Renehan announced his former residence would be converted into a mundane automobile showroom. Plans included the placement of two terra cotta or cement burros at the entrance to Burro Alley, which had been paved three years earlier in 1923.[36]

According to the deed history of the corner, the frontage totaled eighty-six feet facing Palace Avenue on the north and sixty-seven feet facing Burro Alley on the west.[37] Today this corner is the site of the multistoried Bokum Building, built in 1955.[38] To the rear was a small shed, which became the first location in 1953 of today's well-known Shed Restaurant, presently located in Prince Plaza on east Palace Avenue. Lively jazz concerts, promoted by Shed owners Thornton and Polly Carswell, echoed down the narrow alley in 1959.[39]

Burro Alley, once also known as Gertrudis Barcelona Street and Taos Place, where burros waited patiently until their *leñadores*, or firewood-vendor owners, sold and unloaded piñon wood, was closed to automobiles in the year 2003. Fifty years earlier its closing to vehicular traffic was discussed but never accomplished.[40] During World War II government trucks carrying explosives from the train depot on Guadalupe Street to Los Alamos thundered northward, the wrong way, with sirens blaring through the narrow one-way alley.[41] Contrary to popular lore, the site of the famous Palace Restaurant, later known as Señor Lucky, is where the

FIGURE 13. ⊱ Intersection of Burro Alley, Palace, and Grant avenues, Santa Fe, New Mexico. Museum of New Mexico neg. no. 147769.

red-bricked Candelario house once stood, rather than the actual site of Doña Tules's gambling sala.

The fourth building owned by Doña Tules, willed to Refugio and Delfinea Flores, was a long narrow adobe house on the west side of Burro Alley at its entrance to Palace Avenue and immediately south of her residence. At the time of her death in 1852 the house was unoccupied, according to her will. A row of small adobe houses lined the west side of the alley and were demolished in 1930 when the Lensic Theater, today a performing arts theater, was built.[42]

A popular twentieth-century shop, the Square Deal Shoe Shop located on the mid–east side of Burro Alley and owned by David Gallegos, survived for fifty-four years until 1990.[43] Gallegos always enjoyed telling a favorite story to his customers. When his father leased the area he unlocked the front door only to find there was no wooden flooring. Apparently, the previous renter had dug an enormous hole looking for the buried gold of the famous Doña Tules. Joe Gonzales of the adjacent Veterans [sic] Barber Shop rented his space for thirty-eight years, cutting the hair of such famous Santa Fe visitors as Fats Domino.[44]

Burro Alley of today lacks the quaint surroundings and live burros of earlier centuries. Nor has anyone written an authoritative history to date. Palace Avenue was extended into Sandoval Street in the late 1900s, cutting off the alley's north end. Today, French chansons and the smell of freshly baked croissants fill the air. It was painfully lamented in 1926 that "every time a landmark like this [Burro Alley] disappears, we have lost that much more of the celebrity which brings the business which causes them to disappear."[45]

CHAPTER SIX

La Hijuela

~~⁀

La hijuela, or the will, of Gertrudis Barceló, dated October 30, 1850, was written at the time New Mexico became a U.S. territory.[1] It bears her signature in an unsteady hand with seal and rubric. Surprisingly, it is written in English, a language she ostensibly neither understood nor spoke. Witnessed by six prominent New Mexicans and a U.S. Army surgeon, the will identifies the names of her immediate family, friends, servants, and business associates, including that of her last known lover. While revealing a wealth of information, at the same time it leaves many questions unanswered concerning her day-to-day life.

An unprecedented document in nineteenth-century New Mexico history, the Gertrudis Barceló will remains one of the first to be executed by a Hispanic woman in English following the American occupation in 1846. Until this time the Spanish legal system, beginning in the year 1265 with *Las Siete Partidas*, had provided a certain protection for women and their estates. By 1852, at the death of the notorious gambler, laws of the United States applied. Although the Gertrudis Barceló will was dictated

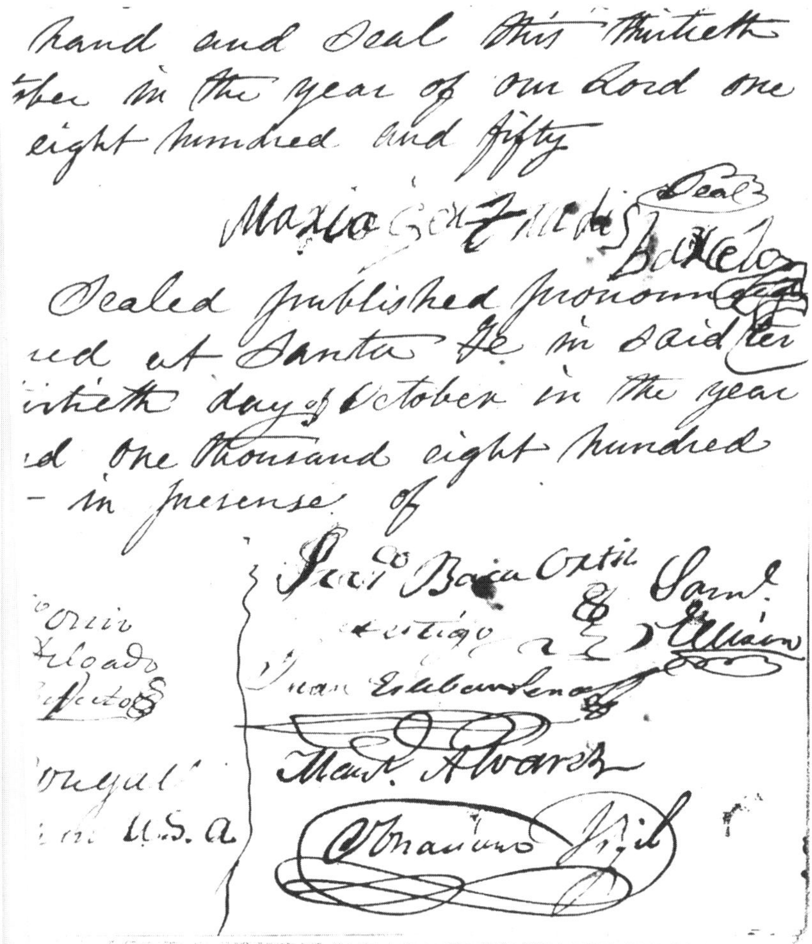

FIGURE 14. ❧ Barceló will signatures, 1850. Author's collection.

in October 1850, not until January 12, 1852, five days prior to her death, was the Last Wills and Testaments Act passed by the New Mexico legislature.

According to sections four to seven, "a verbal [oral] will shall be attested by the same number of witnesses required for the written ones, and besides, two witnesses, there being no more, possessing the same qualifications as required for the written will, to testify that the testator, male or female, was in possession of a sound mind and entire judgment. . . . All wills . . . shall possess uniformity of context in its various parts, the witnesses shall be present, see and hear the testator speak, and each and every one of them shall understand clear [*sic*] and distinctly every part of the will."[2]

Because of its significance, this will, which lists personal and real property belonging to Gertrudis Barceló along with her strong desires concerning its distribution, is published here in its entirety for the first time since she dictated and signed it. Language and spelling remain as found in the original document.[3]

> In the name of God amen. I, Maria Gertrudes Barcelo resident of Santa Fe in the territory of New Mexico being of sound mind and judgement and of the Roman Catholic faith do hereby publish pronounce and declare the following to be my last will and testament. First. I declare and state that I am entirely free from debt and that the property of every kind that I am about to dispose of has been accumulated by my own labor and exertions.
>
> That this my last will and testament is nuncupative [oral] and irrevocable and I wish the substance and clear interpretation intent and meaning thereof to be carried out without reference to any formalities or technicalities of the law.
>
> The disposition which I wish to be made of my property personal and real after my death is as follows (to wit): First. I give and bequeath and devise unto my beloved sister Maria de la Luz Barcelo the house in said town of Santa Fe in which I now reside [written above the line but crossed out—a part of which is at present occupied by American Officers][4] together with all the property therein contained belonging to me including my plate jewelry wearing apparel and household furniture of every kind also my carriage and the land on which said house is situated with all the rights privileges and appurtenances thereto belonging.
>
> Secondly, I give devise and bequeath to Rallitos Gutieras alias Sisnero (a young girl whom I have brought up from infancy and who now resides with me) the house now occupied by Doloris Barcelo in said town of Santa Fe together with the land on which it stands and all the rights privileges and appurtenances thereto belonging to her, the said Rallitos, her heirs and assigns forever in fee simple.

Third. I give bequeath and devise unto Delfinea Flores (daughter of Santiago Flores of said town of Santa Fe) a certain other house which I own and posses in said town (at present unoccupied and west of the land last bequeathed to said Rallitos Gutieras) together with the land on which it stands and the rights privileges and appurtenances thereto belonging to her the said Delfinea her heirs and assigns forever in fee simple.

Fourth. I give and bequeath unto my said sister Maria de la Luz Barcelo and my brother Trinidad Barcelo [inserted above the line—who are my heirs at law] my stock of mules to be equally divided between them one half to each.

Fifth. I give bequeath and devise unto my said brother Trinidad, my said sister Maria de la Luz, and Refugio (the wife of said Santiago Flores) all the money I may possess [inserted above the line—and what may be recovered from those who owe me] at the time of my death, to be divided in equal proportions between them to each one third part of the same after paying my funeral expenses.

Provided that the above devises made hereby to said Refugio and Delfinea Flores are made and given on the express condition that said Santiago Flores shall maintain, educate, clothe, and support the said Rallitos Gutieras and another girl who resides with me called Carmel Sisnero, from the time of my death until they arrive at the age of twenty five years (if not previously married) otherwise to the time of their marriage and no longer.

The above devises are hereby made to the above named parties absolutely and without restriction except as above provided, the land and real property in fee simple, and the personal property absolutely, reserving to the church and government their rights if any they have under the existing laws, to the church fifty dollars for each demand should the existing laws require.

And finally I hereby nominate constitute and appoint Augustus De Marle, Gaspar Ortis, and the reverend Juan Filipe Ortis my executors and charge them to faithfully carry out and perform the forgoing provisions and to conclude, do now again declare publish and pronounce the same to be my last will and testament [inserted above the line—nuncupative and irrevocable] as witness my hand and seal this thirtieth day of October in the year of our Lord one thousand eight hundred fifty.

Seal

/s/ Maria Gertrudis Barcelo

(rubic)

Signed, sealed, published, pronounced, and declared at Santa Fe in said territory this thirtieth day of October in the year of our Lord one thousand eight hundred and fifty in the presence of

Fran^{co} Baca Ortiz

Fran^{co} Ortis	Testigo (rubric)	Saml.
y Delgado	Juan Esteban Sena	Ellison
Prefecto (rubric)	(rubric)	
Chs. McDougall	Man^l. Alvarez	
Surgeon U.S.A.	Donaciano Vigil	
	(rubric)	

[reverse side]   Ma Gertrudes Barcelo

WILL &

TESTAMENT—

Filed in my office

this 24th of June

1852

/s/ J M Giddings

Clk

1852

Territory of New Mexico

County of Santa Fe

I, J M Giddings, Clerk of the Probate Court in and for said County and Territory, do certify that the foregoing last will and testament of Ma Gertrudez Barcelo is hereby copied in Record B page 4, 5, 6, 7 Recorded in my office.

In witness thereof I, J M Giddings, Clerk of said Court have hereto set my hand and affix my private seal there being no seal provided this 19th day May 1852

J M Giddings, Clk

of Probate

(rubric)

Following the signing of her will in 1850, Gertrudis Barceló lived another fourteen and a half months until mid-January 1852. Five months after her death the will was recorded in late June by J. M. Giddings, clerk of the Santa Fe probate court, who was her American son-in-law. Three years later, Santiago Flores and the Reverend José Eulogio Ortíz, half-brother to Vicar Juan Felipe, replaced August de Marle and the Reverend Juan Felipe Ortíz as executors.[5] The appointment of Flores resulted in the two sons-in-law of Doña Tules—Flores and Giddings—exercising more control over her estate than she might have wished during her lifetime.

Diagnosis of a terminal illness more than likely prompted the execution of the will. Early Santa Fean Amado Chaves, whose "prima Amada" (cousin, Amada Baca) or grandmother María Rosa Sisneros, who was a sister-in-law of "doña Tula," confirms this conclusion with his statement, "the doctor who was taking care of her told her that she could not last long."[6] Death certificates requiring the signature of a physician and recording the cause of death were unknown in New Mexico in 1852. But author Ruth Laughlin in her popular novel *The Wind Leaves No Shadow* suggested that Tules suffered from a weak heart.[7]

The orthography of the Gertrudis Barceló will has remained a mystery to historians since it was executed. While there have been some educated guesses made to identify the handwriting, no thorough analysis ever resulted. In 1968, for example, Albuquerque attorney and author Gilberto Espinosa made several astute observations, reaching the erroneous conclusion that early New Mexico historian and witness Samuel Ellison was the author. Espinosa also observed that "its language is not Spanish. I am impressed by those who were in attendance. It indicates Doña Tules was associated with the most distinguished men in Santa Fe at that time."[8]

Espinosa continued, "Without question this Will was written by an American; you [meaning then–state historian Myra Ellen Jenkins] are familiar with many Spanish and Mexican wills of this period and it does not follow that form of language. The Will is well drafted and would pass today. It has its deficiencies which indicate it was not drafted by a finished lawyer." Attorney Espinosa was correct in his belief that the will was written by an American. Contrary to another of his hypotheses, the American writing the will was indeed considered a trained lawyer,

FIGURE 15. ❧ Theodore Dehon Wheaton (1813–73), attorney who wrote the
will of Doña Tules. Author's collection.

who from 1854 to 1858 served as New Mexico's attorney general. After
a careful study of the calligraphy contained in other 1850 documents
held in the New Mexico State Archives with that of the penmanship
of the Gertrudis Barceló will, it becomes evident that the handwriting
belonged to Theodore Dehon Wheaton, an American lawyer with a reputation in Missouri and New Mexico law and politics.[9] Wheaton arrived
in New Mexico with General Stephen Watts Kearny in 1846 at the time

of the U.S.–Mexican War as a private of Captain McMillan's Company D of the Second Regiment of the Missouri Volunteers under Colonel Alexander W. Doniphan.[10]

Further, Wheaton had served as attorney for the ailing Doña one month prior to the writing of her will in 1850, which bolsters the case that he was the will's scribe as well as Doña Tules counsel. The earlier litigation brought by Tules was to collect an unpaid loan in the amount of five hundred dollars against Humphrey and Coulter, proprietors of the United States Hotel.[11]

Perhaps the most remarkable, yet puzzling characteristic of the will is why it was written in English, rather than in Gertrudis Barceló's native tongue of Spanish, the practice indeed unusual for the time. Known to have been a pivotal figure in the forefront of the New Mexican political and social scene of the era, the Doña, who did not possess sufficient ability to fluently speak or write English, might have been making a palpable statement of her pro-American sentiments. From the signatures appearing on the will, there were men present during its execution who were capable of writing it in Spanish. So, unquestionably, the use of English in the document appears intentional, whether by the Doña or by her attorney, Theodore Dehon Wheaton.

Wheaton, the son of a prominent Protestant minister of Trinity Church in Newport, Rhode Island, is described as an "eccentric of retiring nature."[12] He graduated with honors in 1832 from Trinity College in Hartford, Connecticut, and read law with the Honorable Richard K. Randolph of Newport. On the Barceló will, Wheaton made several spelling errors in both English and Spanish, considered not uncommon for the time. And by reason of the will being nuncupative, or oral, the errors possibly resulted from his hasty translation of the legal terminology and oral wishes of Doña Tules from Spanish into English. In 1847 Theodore D. Wheaton, Frank P. Blair, Jr., and Hugh H. Smith, were instrumental in the drafting of the Kearny Code.[13]

By 1850 Wheaton apparently had not totally mastered the Spanish language during his New Mexico residency of slightly over four years. Because he cohabited for a number of years in Taos with a Hispanic woman with whom he had several children, it is likely that he understood and spoke Spanish to a certain level of proficiency.[14] On July 14, 1851, less than nine months following the writing of the Barceló will,

Wheaton was appointed to a commission to prepare a territorial code of law.[15]

Among several other lawyers arriving in Santa Fe with the Missouri Volunteers of the U.S. Army in 1846 at the beginning of the U.S.–Mexican War, Theodore D. Wheaton remained in New Mexico to practice law. He was mustered out of the army to receive the appointment as district attorney for the Second Judicial District at Taos, where in 1847 he had assisted in the prosecution of the assassins of Governor Charles Bent, according to one account. Wheaton later served as Speaker of the House of Representatives of New Mexico Territory and as fifth attorney general. In addition, he was perhaps the first lawyer hired by the Navajo Indians.[16]

The first of three lawyers to pass the Missouri bar following the Platte Purchase in 1840–41, Theodore Wheaton had served in the Missouri legislature before coming to Santa Fe. One Missouri history comments that Wheaton's success in both states was the result "more of tact and shrewdness" than real talent.[17]

Evidenced by her will, Gertrudis Barceló's extended family played a vital role in the life of this influential woman, and she generously remembered the feminine members of her family in the bequests. In contrast, she names her brother Trinidad as the only male heir to benefit from the material fruits of her "labors and exertions," but her husband, Manuel Antonio Sisneros, is not mentioned in the will. Amado Cháves claimed that Sisneros had left Tules earlier, was excommunicated for an unknown reason, and died near Manzano, southeast of Albuquerque. Manuel Antonio is frequently confused with that of his older brother, José Miguel Sisneros."[18]

While still living together as man and wife, the Sisneroses enjoyed a contemporary household arrangement. Manuel Antonio and their servants took care of their adopted daughters whenever the woman gambler was out of town, sometimes for months on end. This proved to be the case for fifteen or more years of their marriage. In general, New Mexico prior to the arrival of the Americans in 1846 had preserved the Spanish concept of conjugal ownership, or *los bienes gananciale*, property acquired during marriage.[19] Had Manuel Antonio remained in Santa Fe as her husband, and provided he had survived her in January 1852, he might have benefited from the numerous responsibilities he would have shouldered, enabling Tules to have a family as well as a career. Throughout the marriage Gertrudis retained her maiden name and control of not only her destiny but her estate.

The beloved younger sister of Tules, María de la Luz, inherited the major portion of the estate—most of which has now been lost to posterity.[20] The light and "somewhat gaudy" carriage carrying the gambler and a beautiful young girl, drawn by three "well fed and spirited mules" described by thespian-writer Matt Field in 1839, has not been found.[21] Apparently, all that remains of Tules's estate today is a *peineta*, or comb; a monte, or gambling table; a *petaca*, or rawhide box; and a silver chalice cup.[22]

Santa Fe probate proceedings mention a "complete inventory" of Tules's estate. Unfortunately, the inventory is now missing from court records. Other historical documents leave a partial paper trail regarding subsequent events following the Doña's death. A listing of additional personal effects belonging to Doña Tules may be found in a civil court case brought in July 1852 by administrators of her estate, Santiago Flores, José Eulogio Ortíz, and Gaspar Ortíz against James M. Giddings. On behalf of the Gertrudis Barceló estate they claimed that the following personal property should be returned by J. M. Giddings: "one large trunk, one small trunk, two large silver dishes, sixteen silver plates, four large silver cups, five small silver cups, two large silver spoons, seven small silver spoons, nine silver forks, one bracero [*brasero*, brazier], one salt cellar and one thousand nine hundred and twenty four dollars of silver coin, of the value of three thousand and fifty four dollars." Finding only one trunk, the U.S. marshal was ordered not to retrieve it from Giddings because no contents were found in it.[23]

Other unforeseen events hindered the final settlement of the estate. On August 2, 1852, seven months following the death of Doña Tules, her residence was burglarized by Pedro Mondragón and Juan Naranjo. Curiously, one court document also listed as one of the burglars the name of Dolores Griego, sister-in-law of Tules and the wife of Trinidad Barceló, who perhaps was an accomplice but did not carry out the actual burglary.[24] The following property was stolen, much of which probably belonged to the monte player during her lifetime:

Four hundred dollars in silver—two rebozos [shawls] the value of fifteen dollars each—one gold cigarero [a *tenaza* or cigarette-tong]

FIGURE 16A. ⚘ Chalice
(*cáliz*, goblet, pewter gold
wash), bequest of Alan
and Ann Vedder (1990.77).
Courtesy of the Museum of
Spanish Colonial Art, Santa
Fe. Photos by author.

FIGURE 16B. ⚘ Travel Chest (*petaca*, nineteenth century), given in memory
of Ruth Laughlin Alexander by her children (1962.99).
Courtesy of the Museum of Spanish Colonial Art, Santa Fe.

the value of fifty dollars—one gold necklace the value of fifty dollars—one gold chain and medal value of fifty dollars—two pair gold earrings the value of ten dollars each—one pair gold earrings the value of five dollars—two finger rings the value of eight dollars each—three finger rings the value of three dollars—one retaculo [*ridículo*, net purse or *relicario*, religious locket] the value of two dollars and one breast pin the value of two dollars.[25]

Bail for burglars Mondragón, Griego, and Naranjo was set at a thousand dollars, five hundred dollars, and five hundred dollars, respectively. They were ordered to appear in court during the next term in September 1852 and "in default thereof to be safely kept in the County jail until discharged by due course of law."[26] Final outcome of the burglary episode is undocumented. During the September 1852 court term, E. J. Barry, clerk of the Second District Court of Taos County, was ordered to file a bill of items against the estate of Gertrudis Barceló. Once again, a list that would be of interest to this story is missing from the probate records.[27]

In death, Tules confirmed her devotion for her younger and widowed sister, who was named the principal beneficiary. A photograph or physical description of María de la Luz presently eludes history. Census records indicate that she was born in Sonora and could neither read nor write.[28] As noted earlier, on November 3, 1822, seventeen-year-old Doña María de la Luz Barceló married Juan Rafael Sanches, son of Manuel Sanches and Gertrudis Chaves of Tomé, New Mexico.[29] Juan Rafael was from a prominent Tajique land-grant family.[30] In the *diligencia*, or interrogation, of the bride and groom, dated October 20, 1822, the bride states that she has resided in Tomé for seven years "since her tender age."[31] This suggests that the Barceló family arrived in Valencia north of Tomé in 1815, which corresponds to within one year of the appearance of the Barceló name in church records.[32]

The four daughters and two sons, recorded as legitimate children of Juan Rafael and María de la Luz, and therefore nieces and nephews of Tules, were María Altagracia de Refugio (b. 1824), María Luisa (b. 1826), José Rumaldo (b. 1828), Victoria (b. 1830), María Teresa de Jesús (b. 1833), and José Vicente (b. 1840). A María Paula, born to *padres no conocidos*, or parents unknown, was baptized "en casa de Rafael Sanchez

FIGURE 17. ❧ Consuelo de los Rayos (Rallitos) Gutierres (1837–1900). Wife
of Lorenzo Labadie and a favorite granddaughter of Doña
Tules. Author's collection.

and Ma. de la Luz Barceló," March 1831. The child died at age nine months
in December 1832.[33]

By the 1850 U.S. census Juan Rafael no longer appeared as a member
of the Sanches household. He has either died of natural causes or has
been killed by Indians. Ten years later María de la Luz, then the wealthi-
est person in the village of Tajique, east of the Manzano Mountains, with
personal and real property valued at $600 and $2,625 respectively, was
living with her adult children and servants.[34] She died January 27, 1885,
at age seventy.[35]

Here begins one of the more intriguing and unsolved mysteries of this story. Rallitos Gutierres alias Sisneros, described in the Barceló will as "the young girl brought up by me [Tules] from infancy," was baptized February 26, 1838, and therefore twelve years old at the writing of the will. Her baptismal record reads, "Maria, daughter of a peon, padres no conocidos." Godparents are Manuel Sisneros and Dolores Griego.[36] Perhaps Tules moved her games out of town at that time and was unable to appear as a *madrina*. María Consuelo de los Rayos, called Rallitos, a popular New Mexico name for girls born between 1833 and 1837, was the

FIGURE 18. ≈ James Madison Giddings (ca. 1813–90). Husband of Petra Gutierres. Author's collection.

illegitimate daughter of Petra Gutierres, who married James Madison Giddings in 1842.[37] Despite family history, Giddings, nevertheless, was not the biological father of Rallitos.

The story of Rallitos and the enigmatic man who fathered her has confounded New Mexicans of later decades, as well as her adoptive family. It was the account of the seduction by Amado Chaves that enticed me to probe further into the remarkable life of Doña Tules. The paradox of a free-spirited woman leading the life of a notorious gambler and mistress, yet a woman of principal protecting at gunpoint the reputation of María Petra I believe to be the romantic intrigue of which great novels and history are made. Chaves's prima Amada gave a description of the window rendezvous at the Barceló Santa Fe residence:

On one occasion when she [Tules] went to Mexico one of the girls had the bad luck to be seduced by one of the Americans who frequented the house. When he had news that she (Dona Tula) was returning he left the country and never returned. In a few months the girl gave birth to a little girl. She made the girl confess who was the father of the child and the girl said who was the father. Dona Tula tried her best [to find] where the man was but never succeeded. During another trip that she made to Mexico the same girl had love affairs with another American. When Dona Tula returned in a few months she noticed that the girl was about to become a mother. She started to watch and saw a man enter the room of the girl by the window. She then went to the house of the priest and requested him to accompany her to her house and told him what she wanted him for. When she left[,] she left a man watching the window and another man at the door. When she and the priest arrived they took their place by the side of the window. She had a pistol in her hand. When the American tried to get out she spoke to him saying that he had to marry the girl and if you do not I will shoot you. The man said that he would marry the girl, to let him go out and he would return to get married. You must get married now or I will kill you. She then called the girl to come to the window and ordered her to light a candle and to come close to the window and the priest married them and left them in holy peace. You known who they were. She raised the little girl but never trusted her to anybody and whenever she went to Mexico she always took the girl with her. And she grew to be a very beautiful girl and became our aunt at law.[38]

Amado Chaves's account is unclear regarding specific details. Petra Gutierres was the girl who was seduced, whether once or twice remains unknown. According to family lore, Petra was said to be an orphan and raised in the Barceló household in Santa Fe.[39] The child born to her in January 1838 as a result of the seduction was Rallitos, also raised by Tules and known for her "big blue eyes" and as a fair-haired beauty. Rallitos, by marrying Lorenzo Labadie, became the aunt-in-law of Amado Chaves.[40] Giddings family history recounts that the several young girls who lived with Tules were always kept locked in their rooms while she played monte into the wee hours of the morning.[41] The shrewd gambler distrusted men and their motives, but judiciously manipulated them to her financial advantage while gambling.

A surviving elderly member of the James Giddings family recounted that Rallitos was believed to be the daughter of Colonel John MacRae Washington, military and civil governor of New Mexico in 1848–49.[42] Born in 1894, Petra Giddings Riddle, the daughter of William Baxter Giddings, and granddaughter of James M. Giddings, related that as children they were taken to a small museum in the east end of the Palace of the Governors and shown a photograph of "Rallitos's father" who was from a "famous Virginia family." The names of "Washington" and "Garrard" lingered in her memory.[43] An early photograph of that room in the Palace shows a portrait of John M. Washington hanging on the wall, just as Petra Riddle recalled. The Amado Chavez account further stated that Doña Tules searched for the father of Petra's child, but never found him. In a major disaster at sea on December 24, 1853, near the mouth of the Delaware River, Colonel J. M. Washington, along with several hundred others, including women, was swept off the deck of the *San Francisco* and drowned. It would appear that only by death could men escape the vengeance of the woman called Tules—that is, of course, if Colonel Washington was indeed the biological father.[44] Lieutenant

FIGURE 19. ❧ Lorenzo Labadie (1825–1904), Indian agent, and C. Gallegos.
        Author's collection.

FIGURE 20. ❧ Petra Giddings Riddle (b. 1894) and Judge Santiago E. Campos (1926–2001), 1985. Granddaughter and great-grandson of James M. Giddings. Author's collection.

Colonel John M. Washington, considered an artillery expert, assisted in the removal of the Cherokee Nation to Oklahoma around 1836 and possibly traveled to New Mexico around that time.

In searching further for the father of Consuelo de los Rayos (Rallitos), I have found two estranjeros who received *guías*, or passports, in Santa Fe on November 12, 1831—"#72 Washington (Knox?) and #74 Washington (Jarrot—Jarret) para Chihuahua and Sonora."[45] The latter name confirms the names recalled by Petra Giddings Riddle, granddaughter of James Giddings; however, the year of 1831 precedes the birth year of Rallitos by six years. Another possibility emerges, that Washington Garrard was a descendant of Governor James Garrard of Kentucky. It may well be that the Giddings family of Rallitos, the favorite granddaughter of Doña Tules, erroneously applied the title of governor to New Mexico's military governor, rather than to another governor such as Governor Garrard of Kentucky.[46] A DNA analysis might solve this long-standing mystery.[47]

Rallitos lived in the Giddings household with her mother and stepfather for only a month following the death of Tules in 1852. She was treated in the same loving manner as the other children of Petra Gutierres

FIGURE 21. ❧ Colonel John MacRae Washington (1797–1853), military and
civil governor of New Mexico, 1848–49. Museum of New
Mexico neg. no. 13116.

and James Giddings, according to Petra Giddings Riddle. Even though he has been identified as Rallitos's father by some historians, Colonel John M. Washington may not have been her father; he was in Florida in 1837, the year of conception of Rallitos.[48] In the fall of 1848 he arrived in New Mexico by way of Chihuahua to become New Mexico's military governor. The question arises, did Washington also have an earlier romantic interlude in Santa Fe in January 1833, the approximate time of the alleged first seduction?[49] To add to this conundrum, a child named María Rosa, parents unknown, was born September 3, 1833, with Manuel Sisnersos and Gertrudis Barceló acting as godparents.[50]

New Mexico society routinely absorbed babies such as Rallitos, María Rosa, and Refugio, born out of wedlock, without necessarily any official adoption being noted in church records. The names of the padrinos may indicate that one or both, if a married couple, godparents adopted the child. It is interesting to note that such births caused no embarrassment among New Mexicans because marriage was difficult, if not impossible, due to the high fee charged by the church. Neither did marriage alone guarantee fidelity on the part of either husband or wife, the woman retaining her maiden name and property, and being legally and sexually free of male dominance.

The many undocumented arrivals and departures of Chihuahua and Santa Fe Trail traders in 1833 and 1837 make the task of paternity identification virtually impossible. One of the early traders in Santa Fe was James M. Giddings, future son-in-law of Tules, who married Petra Gutierres, an adopted daughter and the biological mother of Rallitos. We learn that Giddings was indeed in Santa Fe in 1837.

A month after the death of Tules, fourteen-year-old Rallitos, called "one of the fairest daughters of the territory," married the handsome Indian Agent Lorenzo Labadie on February 16, 1852.[51] On the day of their wedding, and conceivably as a wedding gift, Lorenzo received a commission from Governor James S. Calhoun as colonel of the territorial commission. Rallitos, the favorite of Tules whom she jealously guarded, died at the Giddings fort at Agua Negra, on the west side of the Pecos River near Puerto de Luna on August 10, 1900, at age sixty-two.[52] Petra Giddings Riddle recalled being present at the time of her death.

Delfinea Flores, daughter of Santiago Flores and Refugio Gutierres, was bequeathed the vacant house and property fronting east along

Burro Alley and adjoining the Barceló residence to the south. Nothing is known about Delfinea other than she might have been the María Higinia born October 8, 1847, making her approximately five years old in 1852. Godparents at her baptism were Gertrudis Barceló and Lucius Thruston, presumably a lover of Tules. A professional gambler and trader, he came to New Mexico around 1827 and was appointed Santa Fe prefect between 1846 and 1848 by General Stephen Watts Kearny after the American occupation.[53]

In the will the word *provided*, underlined, precedes the paragraph— "*provided* that the . . . devises made hereby to said Refugio and Delfinea Flores are made and give on the express condition that said Santiago Flores shall maintain educate clothe and support the said Rallitos Gutieras and another girl who resides with me called Carmel Sisneros, from the time of my death until they arrive at the age of twenty five years (if not previously married)."

Believing that Refugio or Delfinea might allow profits from the sale of the real estate to filter into the pockets of Santiago Flores, which ultimately they did seven months after her death, Tules made the gift contingent on his guarantee to care for the girls named.[54] Tules also desired that Rallitos not only be fed and clothed but educated as well, perhaps an important accomplishment lacking in her own life.

Tules's older brother, José Trinidad, was bequeathed money and mules, the two things he probably valued most. Born around 1791 in Sonora, Trinidad, after his arrival in New Mexico married or cohabited with Margarita Dolores Griego of Corrales. Dolores, the legitimate daughter of Francisco Griego and Antonia Montoya, was born in 1806.[55] Trinidad taught school in September 1830 at Cañada de Santa Cruz and was knowledgeable in the businesses of mules and mining.[56] In 1831 María Filomena, five-day-old daughter of Trinidad Barceló and Dolores Griego of San Fernando (near Taos) was baptized by the famous Padre Antonio José Martínez, who opposed the new French bishop Jean Baptiste Lamy for five years. Six-month-old María Filomena died; Padre Martínez buried her in 1832.[57] Santa Fe County records show Trinidad as Santa Fe alcalde in March 1846, five months prior to the American arrival in Santa Fe.

Mexican patriot Trinidad Barceló was charged with treason in 1847, along with several other New Mexicans.[58] He refused to take an oath of allegiance to the United States after the arrival of the Americans, when General Stephen Watts Kearny declared New Mexico to be a part of the United States. After returning to Huásabas, Sonora, following the death of Tules in 1852, Trinidad and Dolores Griego were recorded as baptizing a child there.[59] The date and place of Trinidad's death is unknown, probably in Sonora. Apparently, Trinidad and Dolores had separated prior to her death at age fifty-nine in Albuquerque on December 26, 1865.[60]

Territorial Secretary and Acting-Governor William G. Ritch wrote that, like Tules, Dolores Griego possessed "great natural ability but no education . . . a woman of pluck, perseverance" who would bet at monte while Tules dealt the cards—the odds unquestionably in her favor. Ritch also noted that Dolores was "kept" by an artillery officer under the Mexican government, and "went through a whole campaign against the Navajo Indians."[61] In 1839 Dolores Griego de Barceló reached an oral understanding with a Pedro Sandoval in a controversy over a young girl.[62] Nothing is known about the girl, whether she might have been an adopted child or one of her nieces, Candelaria or Juana Griego, who were living with her in Santa Fe in 1850.[63] Nineteenth-century documents indicate that gambler Dolores Griego accumulated a fairly sizable estate for herself.

Probate clerk James M. Giddings, an American trader from Fayettville, Missouri, and a native of Kentucky, first came to New Mexico from Missouri in 1835. He returned in 1836 and again in 1840, when he became a permanent resident. In 1839 he was a member of the firm of Giddings & Patterson in the Santa Fe trade, and in 1841 of the firm of Giddings & [Nicolas] Gentry on the south side of Santa Fe's plaza.[64] Giddings was baptized into the Catholic Church in March 1842 with El Vicario Juan Felipe Ortíz and Gertrudis Barceló as godparents.[65]

In New Mexico, James Giddings held the positions of clerk of the New Mexico House of Representatives (1847); clerk of the convention (1848); probate clerk of Santa Fe County (1848–52); and clerk of the supreme court (1852–54). As probate clerk in 1852 James M. Giddings recorded the will of Gertrudis Barceló in an elegant and flowing script. He was one of eight men who in July 1851 leased a one-square-mile tract of land of the John Scolly Grant to Colonel Edwin V. Sumner for the ultimate location of Fort Union, New Mexico.[66]

The name of Carmel Sisneros, born around 1836 and approximately the same age as Rallitos, also appeared in the Barceló will. Little is known about this girl other than she was probably a Sisneros relative adopted by Manuel and Tules. In her memoirs, *Shadows of the Past*, Santa Fean Cleofas M. Jaramillo recalled a Carmelita, "who impressed her as a second Tules Barceló."[67] The girl occupied the same gambling sala on El Callejon del Burro in which the "notorious Doña Gertrudes, queen of the gambling den and her companion, Francisca, held sway over governors, generals and other high officials."[68] According to Jaramillo, Carmelita played loud music on her phonograph and enjoyed the company of a magpie and a black cat, both associated with witchcraft. From her American husband she had acquired a knowledge of medicine, thus her title of *la médica*.

Known for her generosity, which was not as ostentatious as that of Doña Tules, Carmelita was said to have fed Anglo, Mexican, and Indian guests alike. The clink of wine glasses and "squeaky" phonograph music, could be heard nightly on narrow Burro Alley. Carmelita claimed that her magpie liked music. A little over a month before Tules died, a Carmel living in the Barceló household married American Enrique [Henry] Derr on December 2, 1851, the son of Ana Marie Setting and Pedro Derr.[69] The girl described by Cleofas Jaramillo seems to fit the Jaramillo description and may well have been the same Carmel Sisneros of the Barceló will.

In the final paragraph of her will, Gertrudis Barceló appointed three executors: August de Marle, Gaspar Ortíz, and the reverend Juan Felipe Ortíz, all well-known figures in nineteenth-century New Mexico history. August de Marle arrived in Santa Fe in 1846 at the time of the U.S.–Mexican War; therefore, he had known Tules for only four years before she appointed him as an executor of her estate. Prior to his arrival with the U.S. Army, de Marle had been the first secretary of the St. Louis Communisten-Verein, a German social movement in the 1840s. In June 1848 he returned to Germany and was a participant of the Democratic Congress (social reformers) in Frankfort-on-Main.[70]

A highly educated man who spoke several languages, August de Marle, according to Acting-Governor W. G. Ritch, was living and gambling with Doña Tules. He became a U.S. citizen in 1851. Following his appointment as one of the executors of the Barceló will, he soon resigned, and in June 1852 sailed for Bremen, Germany.[71] On his return by 1855, the scholarly gentleman August de Marle became clerk of the First Judicial District; in 1856 territorial auditor; in December 1858 public printer; and in 1860 auditor of public accounts. De Marle succeeded Hezekiah S. Johnson as editor of the *Santa Fe Weekly Gazette* on November 19, 1859, after which there was a suspension of publication until May 8, 1860. He also served as the last president of the New Mexico Historical Society before it disbanded due to the Civil War. Born about 1816 in Westphalia, Prussia, August de Marle died in Santa Fe on November 23, 1861, and was buried in an unmarked grave in the old Guadalupe Cemetery on Early Street.[72]

At its April 1860 meeting, eight years after the death of Tules, the New Mexico Historical Society received as a donation from de Marle a clock listed as "a musical clock of curious mechanism." Reporter Matt Field in 1839 described seeing in the sala of Tules "an ornate-but-nonfunctioning American-made clock—the hands of the clock intentionally frozen by the gambler at exactly 6 o'clock, except on holidays when she generously allowed it to run (if indeed it could)."[73] Quite possibly this was the clock mentioned by Field.

Another executor, Gaspar Ortíz y Alarid, the son of Gaspar Ortíz and Dolores Alari(d), served as alcalde, or mayor, of Santa Fe in 1839, an aide-de-camp to Governor Manuel Armijo in 1846, and as captain of the New Mexico militia on the Union side during the Civil War. When Armijo fled from the Americans in 1846, Ortíz was one of three officers who accompanied him to Mexico City. Although trained as a soldier, Gaspar Ortíz was a successful mercantile proprietor who often traveled with his pack trains to Independence, Missouri; Santa Fe; Chihuahua; and Durango, Mexico. Through questionable means he acquired a great deal of property in Santa Fe; following his death, his overwhelming debts resulted in his widow's financial disaster.[74] Gaspar Ortíz y Alarid, for whom the street Don Gaspar is named today, married Magdalena Lucero from Los Luceros north of today's Española. A close neighbor of Gertrudis Barceló, Ortíz y Alarid died July 9, 1882.[75]

The third executor, the Reverend Juan Felipe Ortíz, was the rural dean of La Parroquia when the new bishop Jean Baptiste Lamy arrived in Santa Fe in 1851. From a prestigious New Mexico family and also a conspirator to overthrow the Americans in 1846, he was tried for treason before a military court. Ortíz later became a loyal citizen of the

United States as well as the president of the council of the second legislative assembly of New Mexico Territory.[76]

Witness José Francisco Ortíz y Delgado was born ca. 1810 to Juan Rafael Ortíz and his second wife, Estefana Delgado, therefore a half-brother to Vicar Juan Felípe Ortíz. He married Josefa Baca, daughter of Rafael Baca and María Antonia Martín. To aid in the second establishment of public school in 1825 Don Francisco offered a schoolhouse free of rent to Santa Feans.[77] He was the first alcalde of Santa Fe in 1837 at the time of the Chimayó uprising and administrator of the mails in 1840 and 1841.[78]

The name of Charles McDougall, surgeon, U.S. Army, appears as one of the seven all-male witnesses on the Barceló will.[79] Though a recent arrival in Santa Fe, McDougall was possibly the physician-in-attendance to Doña Tules in 1850, and the one who informed her of the gravity of her illness. Documentation of any diagnosis or treatment by army surgeon McDougall to the woman gambler, a civilian, has not been found. Dr. McDougall remained in Santa Fe from 1850 until August 1852, so more than likely he was also the physician called to the bedside of the dying Doña in January 1852 and may have witnessed her final moments.[80]

A former physician at the U.S. Military Academy at West Point, the forty-six-year-old McDougall arrived in Santa Fe on July 11, 1850, a brief three and a half months prior to witnessing the Barceló will in late October of that year. McDougall had been appointed the new army medical director at Fort Marcy. On arriving in Santa Fe, he was met with a heavy medical schedule, complicated by shortages of medicines in a remote area of the United States.[81]

Surgeon McDougall traveled the Santa Fe Trail from Fort Leavenworth, Kansas, to Santa Fe in the wagon train with the new commanding officer of Fort Marcy, Major Gouverneur Morris, and his wife, Anna Maria. On June 22, 1850, below Middle Spring of the Cimarron Crossing of the Arkansas River, the galloping horseman Francis X. Aubry passed the westbound Morris caravan, which included Third Infantry officers and families. Missouri-bound Aubry, called the "Skimmer of the Plains," traveled a record 125 miles in twenty hours, meeting about four hundred traders' wagons en route to Santa Fe.[82]

Anna Maria DeCamp Morris, the daughter of an army surgeon, in her diary of the trip to New Mexico in 1850, frequently wrote about the charming Dr. Charles McDougall, declaring him to be her "excellent

FIGURE 22. ❧ Dr. Charles McDougall (1804–85), Fort Marcy physician and
surgeon, Santa Fe. Courtesy of National Library of Medicine,
Bethesda, Maryland, neg. no. 87-1.

friend."[83] After a social call by the doctor in Santa Fe, she recorded that
he was "a personable gentlemanly man." On the tedious eight-hundred-
mile Santa Fe Trail journey westward, the doctor provided coveted gifts
of fresh food on the trail for Anna Maria's dinners, which included "a
little heifer," "a Golden Plover," and "some nice little fish." The bon vivant

McDougall even mixed an eggnog to toast the fourth of July 1850 near Wagon Mound, New Mexico.

Other gestures made to Anna Maria courtesy of Dr. McDougall were champagne and the use of the beautiful new carriage he had purchased before leaving Fort Leavenworth. The doctor was adept at wooing the ladies and quite obviously enjoyed feminine company. On his arrival in the West, the Ohio-born physician attended the local bailes with the dark-eyed señoritas of New Mexico.[84] Apart from the fandangos, social life, and many attractive Santa Fe women, McDougall initially wished to be moved to another post more to his liking, such as Fort Snelling, where he was formerly stationed.[85] Little did he know that by remaining in Santa Fe he would become a part of history by taking the pulse of the famous-but-ailing Doña Tules. Dr. Charles McDougall's arrival in Santa Fe in midsummer of 1850 proved too late for him to have known the notorious woman gambler in her prime, a femme fatale who was an exceedingly intelligent charmer of men during her zenith.

Dr. McDougall enjoyed an excellent reputation in Kansas as a competent surgeon in any emergency. In 1850, prior to this Santa Fe Trail trip, the mother-in-law of a Captain Alexander B. Dyer was cut across the face with an ax. The assailant, a slave wanting her freedom, was apparently aiming at her owner's neck but instead struck her just below the eyes, the deep cut severed both jawbones. McDougall, then stationed at Fort Leavenworth, attended the brutal wound of the patient, who happened to be the great-granddaughter of Major John Trigg, an artillery officer under General George Washington.[86]

The doctor's expertise extended to childbirth as well, according to young Catherine Bowen. In early 1852, following the death of Tules, the wife of a soldier stationed at Fort Union, New Mexico, wrote:

> Doct. McDougal an old and experienced surgeon attended me and I was not right hard sick more than an hour, though I had been grumbling all during the day. . . . In the morning I made out a few mince pies and boiled custard for company that dined with us at 4 o'clock.[87]

Francisco Baca y Ortíz, known as "El Ciudadano," was another witness whose signature and rubric appeared on the Doña Tules will in

1850. He was born about 1795 to Juan Domingo Baca, a captain at the Santa Fe presidio, and his second wife, Ana Gertrudis Ortíz. Witnesses Baca y Ortíz and Ortíz y Delgado were elected members of the second Territorial Deputation in October 16, 1826. Governor Manuel Armijo in 1827 dissolved the Santa Fe *ayuntamiento*, of which Francisco Baca was a member, because all were related to one another. By 1833 Baca y Ortíz was commandant of the Real de Dolores garrison and the first alcalde of Santa Fe. In 1836, he lived near the Río Chiquito al Puente de Guadalupe, and in 1837 he was again appointed Santa Fe alcalde.[88] Indeed a powerful man, Baca y Ortíz died before 1869.[89]

Witness Samuel Ellison was born February 22, 1817, in Kentucky of Swedish and German heritage. At age twenty he moved from Kentucky to Cincinnati, Ohio, where he served under Colonel William T. Sherman with the rank of lieutenant. Ellison traveled to Houston where he remained in Texas until 1842, when he crossed the Rio Grande into Mexico. In 1848 he came to Santa Fe with Colonel John Washington as quartermaster's agent, and in 1849 was employed as interpreter and secretary to Colonel John Munroe, then civil and military commandant of New Mexico. Ellison was appointed secretary, translator, and interpreter for William Carr Lane, who succeeded James S. Calhoun as governor, and acted in the same capacity for governors David Merriwether and Abraham Rencher. Ellison served in the New Mexico legislature in 1856, 1865, and 1866, when he was speaker of the house in the fifteenth assembly. In 1859 Ellison was appointed clerk of the Supreme Court and of the First Judicial District court of the territory, resigning in 1866, and appointed territorial librarian in 1881. Ellison died July 21, 1889.[90]

From an old New Mexican family, Juan Esteban Sena married Rosario Alarid. He operated a store on the southwest corner of the plaza during the time that merchant James Josiah Webb was in Santa Fe from 1844 to 1847. Webb declared it to be the second-best store to that of John Scolly, the difference being that Scolly's store had a planked floor, one of perhaps only two or three in the territory at the time.[91] Don Juan Esteban, the father of Major José Doroteo Sena, commissioned the casting of a "good sized" bell which adorned the Sena private chapel on upper Palace Avenue, later the home of L. Bradford Prince.[92]

A prominent name in New Mexico nineteenth-century history was that of Spaniard Manuel Alvarez. Born in 1794 in Abelgas, Spain,

Alvarez at age twenty-four sailed to Mexico from Spain in 1818, where he remained until 1823–24. From Mexico via Havana to New York, he arrived in St. Louis, Missouri, a bustling center for fur trappers. The lure of the fur trade motivated him to join François Robidoux and his entourage to trap in New Mexico. In 1824 he opened a store in Santa Fe, a few years following the opening of the Santa Fe Trail trade. After five or so years Alvarez joined the American Fur Company on the Upper Missouri, along with David Dawson Mitchell, an early bourgeois at Fort Union. By 1839 and fluent in Spanish, French, Latin, and English, Alvarez was appointed third U.S consul and commercial agent in Santa Fe. In 1846 Manuel Alvarez and Lieutenant Colonel Mitchell would meet again in Santa Fe with the arrival of the Army of the West at the outset of the U.S.–Mexican War.[93]

Alvarez died July 6, 1856, in Santa Fe. His funeral expenses were substantial, equaling those of Doña Tules, who had died four years earlier. Apparently, his body was taken by wagon down El Camino Real de Tierra Adentro and then eastward to Monterrey, Mexico. A contemporary and business associate of Doña Tules, Manuel Alvarez's death was recorded in the archives of the Archdiocese of Santa Fe. The entry is signed by the French priest Etienne M. Avel, listing Charles [Blümner?] and José Mercure as witnesses.[94] Curiously, no place of burial in Santa Fe, such as the parroquia or its camposanto, appears. Even more extraordinary are the facts surrounding the mysterious burial and lashing of Alvarez's body in Monterrey.[95]

It is not known if Manuel Alvarez was an hermano, or member, of a flagellant brotherhood in Spain or New Mexico, which might explain the scourging, thought by the brotherhood to be beneficial for the soul.[96] However, the new bishop Jean Baptiste Lamy and various other members of the church hierarchy would not have allowed this kind of penance.[97] The details of the covert burial and postmortem lashing presently remain unknown.[98]

A contemporary of Manuel Alvarez was Donaciano Vigil. Born in 1802, Vigil was first appointed secretary of the territory in August 1846, then governor in 1847 by General Stephen Watts Kearny after the brutal assassination of Governor Charles Bent in Taos. A man of rather duplicitous reputation, the educated Vigil miraculously emerged on the winning side no matter the circumstance. During the 1837 Santa Cruz uprising against Governor Albino Pérez, Donaciano escaped death, was acquitted of cowardice, acquired army rank, and acted as military secretary to Governor Manuel Armijo until 1843. He died August 11, 1877.[99]

It is from the important names listed as executors and witnesses in the Barceló will that we can infer the significance of Gertrudis's life as a woman of extraordinary business acumen and social standing in the Santa Fe community. She entrusted her wealth to those she charged to carry out her wishes faithfully. Regarding trustworthiness, nevertheless, the most revealing statement casts a shadow on her trust of her son-in-law, Santiago Flores.

CHAPTER SEVEN

Vita fugit sicut umbra —
Life fleeth like a shadow

～🜪

On the wintry morning of Saturday, January 17, 1852, a sweet blue haze of piñon smoke wreathed Santa Fe.[1] Scarcely had the newly appointed vicar apostolic cleaned the jornada dust from his shoes following his mandatory trip to Durango, Mexico, when the bells of the old parish church tolled the death of an important person in the community.[2] The famed Gertrudis Barceló had received the last rites of the church before her death on the advice of her *comadre*, Doña Guadalupe Tafoya, a devout Catholic who believed it better to confess and be forgiven as a safe passport to the hereafter rather than risk eternal damnation.[3]

Doña Gertrudis Barceló carefully planned the events of her funeral just as she had the course of her entire adult life. With the anticipated assurance of salvation by having New Mexico's first bishop, later archbishop, presiding over her Mass and burial inside the hallowed church walls, eternal damnation seemed remote. Hadn't she given money to the poor by tossing gold pieces from her carriage, as legend told, and religiously cared for the fatherless children of her family, who were faithfully baptized into the church? She was received into the highest circles of Santa Fe society, which in itself might be considered an affirmation of her character and charitable deeds in Santa Fe. Surely, past transgressions in questionable professions to avoid poverty might be forgiven. The savvy woman gambler clung to that belief to the end of her celebrated life.

The grand finale to the life and career of Gertrudis Barceló as wife, mother, grandmother, gambler, madam, entrepreneur, musical patroness, heroine, and spy would proceed as she had envisioned it—her mortal and stylishly dressed remains *à la costume de mort* surrounded by mourning family and friends. Flickering *velorio* candles surrounding the dead Doña in her Burro Alley–Palace Avenue home cast an aura of serenity before guttering out in a stream of smoke as the melancholy singing of the *alabados* ceased.[4]

An early New Mexico custom, the velorio, or wake, was composed of prayers for intercession of the different saints for the repose of the ancestral souls of those present. Ancestors of those attending are mentioned by name perhaps as far back as great-great-grandparents. Close to midnight the rosary was repeated, after which supper is served to all those attending the wake. Chile was the main dish, thus the reason young people refer to a wake as *el chillito*. Not to attend a velorio and funeral was considered disrespectful to the memory of the deceased, an unforgivable *yerro*, or gaffe.[5]

According to returning Santa Fe Trail traders in December 1852, the weather was very severe with "a great depth of snow on the plains."[6] The frozen ground of the ancient streets in Santa Fe was swept clean by *trabajadores* with primitive *escobas*, or brooms, a minor expense of the costly funeral.[7] Hungry mongrels cowered among the onlookers lining the funeral route from lower Palace Avenue to the eastern end of San Francisco Street. The mud Parroquia, or parish church, faced westward down the road dedicated to St. Francis, the route of El Camino Real de Tierra Adentro from Chihuahua. El Camino Real converged with the Santa Fe Trail at the southeast corner of the *plaza constitutional*. And, if only for a moment perhaps, gamblers at the monte tables of the old Fonda ceased their betting to recall La Doña Tules, known to have been the most expert monte dealer who ever played the game.

Led by a parishioner carrying a tall cross followed by priests, a solemn

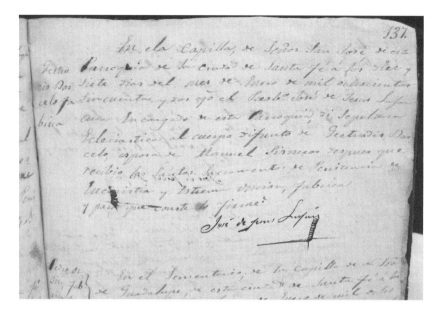

FIGURE 23. ❧ Burial entry of La Parroquia (parish church) of Doña Tules.
Courtesy of the Archives of the Archdiocese of Santa Fe.

and elaborate procession of *familia* and *ciudadanos*, family and citizens,
left the Barceló residence to walk the four or five blocks to La Parroquia,
the parapets of its walls yet uncrenellated by French taste.[8] During the
many *pasos*, or intermittent stops, priests prayed for the Doña's departed
soul; the richer the deceased, the greater the number of pasos, believed
by some to be a display of vanity rather than religious significance. Use
of the tall cross rather than a short one, the thurible and incense, and
the extra mourners all became symbols of the deceased's prestige in the
community. An exhausting and repetitive ritual for those carrying the
linen-draped coffin, the body of Santa Fe's most famous woman was
lowered to the ground time after time, then again lifted to the carriers'
shoulders after each stop.[9]

Unquestionably, one of the grandest of all nineteenth-century Santa
Fe funeral processions, with the exception perhaps of Archbishop Jean
Baptiste Lamy's thirty-plus years later in 1888, skirted the portal of El
Palacio, the governor's palace since 1610.[10] A cortège of black-robed
priests, black-shawled women, and uniformed Mexican and American

soldiers slowly threaded its way through the narrow streets. Strangely, no gold coins were tossed to the *pobladores*.[11] Bells continued tolling until the arrival of the procession at the church as the heavy doors of La Parroquia opened wide for the final time to receive the mortal remains of the legendary Gertrudis Barceló.

Among the sedately clothed priests leading the procession was Father José de Jesús Luján, pastor of La Parroquia, who made the burial entry with his unique rubric in church records for María Gertrudis Barceló, *esposa* de Manuel Sisneros.[12] Father Luján was adept at planning ostentatious events. On this occasion apparently the good Father did not remove his surplice in a display of grief for the deceased as he walked through the streets, as he was known to have done earlier. The new French bishop was in town. The deceased gambler in 1852 might have valued earthly power over religious power. In fact, she would have prized more the removal of plumed military hats as her coffin passed, or the bowed, feverish head of New Mexico's first civil territorial governor. The ailing James Silas Calhoun died five months later on the Santa Fe Trail and was buried on the waterfront of the Town of Kansas (Kansas

FIGURE 24. ❧ La Parroquia (parish church), Santa Fe, New Mexico, ca. 1876. Photo by Nicholas Brown (half of stereoscopic view). Museum of New Mexico neg. no. 10059.

FIGURE 25. ❧ Padre José de Jesús Luján (ca. 1812–85), 1880–81, Santa Fe,
New Mexico. Photo by W. Henry Brown. Museum of
New Mexico neg. no. 9980.

City, Missouri), to be forgotten for the next century. Such public display for Doña Tules would acknowledge her past prominence in the Santa Fe community and her distinction among the military and *gente fina* of Mexico and New Mexico.

The obsequies of this ill-famed woman were an event to be recorded in history. And they were—in many national newspapers, including the *St. Louis Republican* and the *New York Daily Tribune*. Other comments appeared as well about the ostentatious funeral. Twenty-four-year-old Horace L. Dickinson, known for ridiculing Hispanics, wrote to his friend Edward Kern: "Old Madame Toolis is dead and such a funeral I never saw. Bishop, five priests, music, candles, *estaciones* &c, cost $1600.00—$1,000 for the Bishop and the rest divided around. I believe Uncle Jim Giddings [son-in-law of Doña Tules] is somewhat the gainer by the event. I hope so anyhow."[13]

A description of the Barceló funeral was published by the biased W. W. H. Davis in his *El Gringo*. In a rare charitable moment Davis credited the Mexican people with being "a peaceful and quiet race, mild and amiable . . . easily governed if treated with kindness and justice."[14] Another puritanical denunciation appeared in the diary of Bishop Josiah Cruickshank Talbot of the Northwest Diocese of the Protestant Episcopal Church, who called Bishop Lamy's conduct in the matter "utterly disgraceful." Anglican Talbot was further shocked by New Mexico's "loose morals," "universal concubinage," and "open adultry [*sic*]" in which "priests and people alike indulged."[15]

Despite such condemnation, Doña Tules's fame reached far and wide among the gambling Santa Fe and Chihuahua Trail traders who visited New Mexico in the 1830s and 1840s. Moreover, her demise would be of interest to newspaper readers across the country and even on the other side of the Atlantic Ocean. Though often discounted by historians, commentaries on the funeral are unsurprisingly repetitive, one newspaper copying another. Should we then believe that the funeral expenses listed in the account below came from the original so-called "bishop's bill," now missing from the Santa Fe probate court records?[16] The writer of the following article remains yet unidentified:

> Among the *memorabilia* of Santa Fe for this month may be reckoned the death of Dona Gertrudes Barcelo, otherwise known as

Madame Tules. She has been celebrated by Gregg in his sketches, and is known to all Americans, who have known anything of New Mexico for the last quarter of a century. Of poor and humble origin in Sonora, she came into New Mexico when young, and by a certain sprightliness of intellect and force of character, though like nearly all the Mexican women, totally illiterate, she attained the distinction, whatever that may be worth, of being the most famed of her sex in her adopted home. At her decease, years had told upon her constitution less than the course of her life. She took early to two professions common in this country of easy morals. The days and nights which she spent, as a successful gamester, the presiding divinity of the monte table, are uncounted; so also is the number of her various *amantes*.

In compliance with her directions, no expense was spared upon her funeral; and she had the honor of being the first person in New-Mexico, who was ever buried by a Bishop. All the New-Mexican magnificance of the gorgeous Church to which she belonged was in requisition on this occasion. Her coffin, richly bound and lined, and draped with costly silk and lawns [fine linen] was surrounded by a company of religious functionaries splendid in their laced and gilded attire, with chanters singing and censers swinging, and followed by a concourse of persons, each holding a lighted wax candle, the whole forming a galaxy which at night would have made a very imposing illumination. The interior of the Church was twinkling with a multitude of the same kind of lusters, which presented a striking spectacle.

The repose of the departed soul was assured by the appropriate rites, in the present case prolonged for hours; and the interment of her remains, which took place in one of the chapels attached to *La Santa Iglesia Parroquial*, was followed by a homily from the Bishop, in which the speaker addressed the crowd in Spanish, besides dwelling upon the importance of the services of the Church, enforced the necessity of a Christian life.

The expectations of the deceased, who had provided for costly obsequies, were not disappointed. The sum total of the following expense account of the funeral will be apparent to many of your readers, who may not comprehend the items:

Los derechos del Senor Obispo, por el funeral de la Senora
Gertrudes Barcelo $1,000
    JUAN LAMY, Vico. Apolor de N. Mejico.
    Santa Fe, 17 de Enero, 1852.
Cuenta del funeral de la finada Gertrudes Barcelo
        Posos [pasos] .... $150[17]
        Derechos del cura 100
        Fabrica 50
        Sepulcro 50
        Acompanar los 250
        Cantores 12
        Organista 30
        Monarcias 3
        Encenias 2
        Dalmatica 2

               ———

               $649
       Jose de Jesus Lujan
      Santa Fe, Enero 17, 1852.

To this amount should be added whatever may have been
expended for candles, drapery, &c., &c., a sum not less, probably than four hundred dollars; and the total will be found to
exceed two thousand dollars.

An explanatory footnote at bottom of newspaper column continued:

As many of our readers may not understand the terms used in
    the above, we add the following explanations.
Posos [pasos]-Son los vezes que paraba el cuerpo.
Halts-Are the times the procession halts, and the priests per-
    form a ceremony round the corpse.
*Fabrica-Derechos que corresponden al fabriquero por examinar
    el sepulcro.*
Marking out the grave-Fees paid to the person who does it.
A *Fabriquero* is one who is charged with the care of parish
    buildings.
Sepulcro-Es un donde se deposite el cuerpo del defuncto.

Grave.

Acompanar los

Accompaniment of religious functionarie—attendant priests.

Cantore-Para alivio el descanso del alma.

Chanters-For the relief and rest of the departed soul.

Organista-Es uno que toca el organo.

Organist.

Monarcias-Son los miembres que sirven a la iglesia.

Lesser servants of the church.

Encenias-Son los que usaban son los monarcias, fabriqueros.

Ensignia of Santa Fe-Carried by the lesser servants and church-
goers.

*Dalmatica-Derecho del vestido de la iglesia en la practica del
servicio divino*

Catolica Romano.

A kind of vestment [an open-sleeved tunic].[18]

With New Mexican pomp and circumstance, the fifty-one-year-old
Gertrudis Barceló was laid to rest in La Capilla de San José de Padua
in La Parroquia beside her ten-month-old granddaughter, María Rosa
Bersabe, who was buried in 1847.[19] Between 1834 and 1852 twelve burials in the church occurred, the last being that of Doña Tules. A *fábrica*
(burial cost) of thirty-two pesos and four reales was paid to the church
for one-year-old Rosa's burial in the south chapel dedicated to San José.
Rosa Genobeva Bersabe was the daughter of trader Santiago Flores and
Doña Refugio Sisneros, the Chihuahua son-in-law and adopted daughter of the deceased gambler. Tules, along with an American named
"don Enrique Coles," had served as Rosa's godparents at her baptism in
June 1846.[20]

According to the listed expenses of Gertrudis Barceló's funeral, the
traditional guitar and violin played by local musicians described by
army lieutenant J. W. Abert in 1846 were abandoned for the more religious sound, at least to French ears, of a small reed organ or melodeon.
Lieutenant Abert commented: "I was much surprised with the manners
of the Mexicans at a funeral. They marched with great rapidity through
the streets near the church, with a band of music. The instruments were
principally violins, and these were played furiously, sending forth wild

raging music . . . and the mourners talked and laughed gaily, which seemed to me most strange. I was told, too, that the tunes played were the same as those which sounded at the fandango."[21]

Pancho's band with a Mexican harp accompaniment, brought to Santa Fe at the request of Doña Tules, was nowhere to be heard.[22] Bishop Lamy had purchased the Parroquia pump organ from a friendly Protestant minister named Gustavo Antonio Noël while en route to Santa Fe from San Antonio in 1851. The organist's fee noted for the funeral Mass of Tules was possibly paid to Noël or an organist named Augustine Hayne, a Lutheran who played an organ in the Castrense (military chapel) in 1854.[23] This change of musical instruments used during the Mass proved to be only the first salvo of many reforms yet to come in Lamy's bishopric.

La Parroquia had no seats or pews except possibly a few chairs for the Mass, provided mainly for the few Americans who were Catholic. According to two nineteenth-century Protestant women visitors, "Mexican parishioners knelt or sat on the hard, cold floor" and "the women kneeled all over the floor . . . while the men stood up."[24] Priests robed in their heavy vestments, traditionally worn throughout the centuries for warmth in unheated churches, suffered far less from the cold, adobe building than their captive audience of several hours. The mud roof spanning the long one-hundred-twenty-one-foot by a narrow twenty-two-foot nave continued leaking until the mid-1880s.[25] Prior to the building of St. Francis Cathedral, Bishop Lamy used an umbrella under which to give his homily in order to protect his ornate French vestments during the few rainy months in Santa Fe.

La Capilla de San Antonio de Padua, the south chapel in which Gertrudis Barceló was buried, was donated around 1796 by the wealthy patrón Don Antonio José Ortíz. In return for his generosity he requested that the church allow him and his family to be buried there, which was granted.[26] By late 1852 following the burial of Gertrudis Barceló, the adobe chapel's disrepair reached a crucial point and reconstruction began. Santa Fe Trail trader J. M. Kingsbury wrote to Josiah J. Webb in July 1853 that not only had the tower of their Protestant church under construction collapsed, but "about the same time the end of the Bishop's new Chapel fell out, showing that their faith & chapels are no stronger than ours."[27]

Clearly, La Capilla de San José underwent several alterations, though in 1850 near the time of the Barceló funeral it still retained the large altar screen donated by Antonio José Ortíz.[28] By 1894 the chapel had lost twelve feet at its inner or north end, when it temporarily became a museum until 1902. Between 1912 and 1932 the exterior wall received a territorial-style brick coping and was rededicated to St. Anthony of Padua, ultimately changed to the name by which it is known today, the Chapel of the Good Shepherd. An eighteenth-century "picture" by Pasquale Veri of Christ in Gethsemane hung on a wall of the St. Anthony chapel during the early twentieth century.[29]

What happened to the remains of the legendary Gertrudis Barceló? It appears the same unfortunate aftermath that occurred with several other burials in the chapel—demolition by hasty construction workers ignoring any archaeological analysis of human remains that might have been found.[30] The Parroquia's small nave remained intact another thirty-two years while the stone walls of the larger Romanesque cathedral rose stone-by-stone over and around it. The new walls erroneously replicated the ancient building's inaccuracies; the nave was not a true rectangle but converged near the altar, similar to other early New Mexican churches. By retaining the old church within the new the parishioners might continue worshipping uninterrupted until the mud walls of La Parroquia were demolished by one hundred men in 1884, the mud adobes used for surfacing a nearby street.[31]

In desperate need of money to carry out the many pressing obligations of the geographically isolated vicariate with crumbling mud churches, Lamy buried Gertrudis Barceló inside La Parroquia, possibly out of humbling necessity. Soon, however, he would be questioned by a reporter:

> Since the return from Durango of Bishop Lowry [sic] I have had the pleasure of an interesting conversation with him. He describes all of northern Mexico, which he saw, Sonora, Chihuahua, and Durango, as in a most distressed and pitiable condition. Cholera and drought, with its consequence of famine, have severely scourged that country; but its most terrible and fatal enemy is the Indians. The Apaches and Comanches, especially the latter, may now fairly call the country their own. . . .

Some criticism had been made upon the large amount paid on occasion of Gertrudes Barcalo's [*sic*] funeral. But it should be understood that all such expenses are at the option of the parties paying them; and that the sum paid to the Bishop on this occasion was treated as a gift to the church, and will be applied to the re-edification of the church here known as La Capilla Castrense.[32]

FIGURE 26. ❧ Archbishop Jean Baptiste Lamy (1814–88). Museum of New Mexico neg. no. 35878.

Regarding Lamy's candid response, Fray Angélico Chávez wrote that heretofore the priest received his livelihood from stipends, fixed by the bishop's *arancel*, or list of fees, and earned from Mass intentions, baptisms, marriages, or funerals. Tithes of grain or sheep amounted to a pittance, and from 1777 on New Mexicans avoided paying either if possible.[33] Obviously, nothing was ever mentioned about any costly new construction, which was expected to come from the pocket of a rich donor.

In 1852 contemplation of the repair of La Castrense, also called the Chapel of Our Lady of Light and on the south side of Santa Fe's plaza, or a major construction project such as St. Francis Cathedral, begun in 1869, was beyond economic or physical comprehension. Few stonemasons capable of building so massive a structure lived in New Mexico. Master craftsmen had to be brought from Europe, another expense, and the infrastructure for the unprecedented construction established. But Lamy knew from the outset of his less-than-momentous arrival in New Mexico in 1851 that churches and teachers would be his most immediate priorities. Consequently, the 1852 death of Gertrudis Barceló was a providential happenstance that accomplished at least one of Lamy's goals, albeit only a temporary one—the restoration of La Castrense.

Within six months following the Barceló funeral, Lamy made the eight-hundred-mile journey to Missouri and Kentucky on his first of many trips across the Santa Fe Trail. Before leaving the North American continent he had left word in Kentucky for the Sisters of Loretto to accompany him on his return and to teach in New Mexico.[34] In the fall of 1852 he triumphantly returned to New Mexico with both money and teachers, who were struggling to learn the Spanish language while traveling the Santa Fe Trail. Their school was delayed a year in opening to insure their Spanish was equal to the task before them. Even as Lamy left Santa Fe for Durango in the fall of 1851 construction on La Castrense had already begun under the supervision of his seminarian friend and vicar general, Projectus Machebeuf.[35] The dramatic physical and liturgical changes immediately initiated by Bishop Lamy on his arrival give us insight to his dedication to his bishopric.

The same day as the pretentious funeral of Gertrudis Barceló, Father José de Jesús Luján, who called himself "el cura encargado," or "priest in charge," of the Parroquia, performed a wedding: José Romero was united in marriage with María Ignacia Martines. Due only to the coincidental date of their wedding on January 17, 1852, the same day as the funeral of Doña Tules, their names are now a part of nineteenth-century Santa Fe history.[36]

Little is known about the construction project of the old military chapel known as La Castrense between 1852 and 1859, when it was finally sold and traded to merchant Simón Delgado.[37] Bishop Lamy initially planned to keep the chapel at the time of the Barceló funeral, when he encountered an artist by the name of William James Hinchey in the Louvre in Paris. Lamy encouraged and possibly financed the artist's travel to Santa Fe.[38] In 1854 Hinchey wrote a total of seventeen diaries in Pitman shorthand, which were transcribed by his descendant Stephen in December 1957. Bishop Jean Baptiste Lamy met Irishman Hinchey as the student-artist was copying religious paintings of the old masters. Hinchey's diary concerning the Our Lady of Light Chapel (La Castrense) sheds significant new light on its history. It is doubtful that the Irish artist ever heard of the woman whose money may have paid his expenses to travel to New Mexico. Hinchey recorded his artistic endeavors, which were soon demolished along with the chapel.[39]

William James Hinchey left Santa Fe on Wednesday, February 28, 1855, to return to Missouri via the Santa Fe Trail. Though the gambler named Gertrudis Barceló never crossed the Santa Fe Trail, with her death and burial a turbulent era came to an end. The name of Gertrudis Barceló, called Doña Tules, still lingers at the intersection of Burro Alley and Palace Avenue. It might please her to know that her name may be found today in the New York Public Library and many others. Additionally, a number of novels, a play, and a musical, performed during "Expo 92" in Seville, Spain, have been written about her. And now this, her biography, two hundred years and more after her birth.[40]

In the Spanish tradition Doña Tules knew how to die well. Her legend lives on. And as Mark Twain might admonish us, "Why ruin a good story with truth?"

Appendix A

In 1846, D. D. Mitchell wrote the following letter to a St. Louis friend, Judge R. Wash, near the time he was courting Doña Tules for the thousand-dollar loan to feed and equip his Chihuahua Rangers. The letter gives a military view of the sentiment on Santa Fe and the U.S.– Mexican war at the time.

Lt. Col. David Dawson Mitchell, Santa Feé, to R. Wash, St. Louis, Mo., Octr 17, 1846.[1]

Dear Judge,

This being Sunday and having gotten thro' with my long letter to Chin[?] I concluded to kill off the balance of a long day by scribling something in the shape of a letter to you.

To begin with, I am thoroughly disgusted with the country, and the whole expedition. The govt. did not carry out the promises made to [Sterling] Price and his regiment because it would conflict with *previous* instructions, and authority given to Genl [Stephen Watts] Kearny: consequently the whole regiment and "battalion" will be left here in New Mexico in a state of "masterly inactivity" during the winter and spring. Donaphon's regiment has been ordered to Chihuahua and will start in a few days. Price has *permission* from Gen^{l-}to proceed on to California with a force not exceeding 500 mounted men: and in the event of his going, I am assigned to the command of the troops in New Mexico.

Price is sick, and disgusted—throws out occasional threats against [President] James K. Polk and others; and it is now doubtful whether he will go to California or not. In the event of his not going, I have applied for orders to proceed on south with all the mounted troops in the country—consisting of 1,500 men—including Maj. [Meriwether Lewis] Clark's battalion of artillary.[2] If this authority is given to me (and I have the promise of it) I shall go as far south as practicable and get up a fight if possible. Toward spring I will pick out some route thro' Texas and strike the Mississippi at the most convenient point, and from thence get home in a few days. This is a brief sketch of what I *expect* to do. What will be the result, time only can determine.

There is one thing however certain—if I go south in command of 1500 men I will kick up a devil of a dust and leave our *loco* administration to settle the matter the best way they can.[3] They have acted the fool in the whole matter and I am determined to join in playing out the game.

Genl Kearny has gone on to California with two companies of Dragoons and the Mormon Battalion—500 men—will leave tomorrow under command of Capt. [Philip St. George] Cook to follow in his footsteps.[4] What the d'l [devil] they are going for would defy a Yanky to guess as Lt. Col. [John C.] Fremont aided by the Pacific Squadron has already taken possession of the country, and done *all* that Genl K was ordered to do.[5] Fremont is Gov. pro-tem and I suppose during the present session of Congress he will be made brevet brig Genl and Commandant of as much of Mexico *as we can take*! So much in the shape of military news: a word will describe the country and I cant do it better than by repeating the words of a volunteer—a very respectible Missouri farmer.

The day before we entered Santa Fé I had put him on detached service to drive my baggage wagon and while we were at dinner he walked up to the camp fire to light his pipe: "Col" said he "what do you think of this country?" I answered his question Yanky fashion by asking what *he* thought of it. "Why Sir"—he replied—"I begin to believe in them old bible stories. The bible says that it took God almighty six days to make the world, and that on the seventh he rested. Now *I* never believed a word of this before, but now I do and all this region after you cross the Arkansas was made late Saturday morning when he was d [amn]ed tired *and in a bad humor at that*!" I threw off my military dignity for the time being, and gave the fellow a glass of grog for his philosophy.

The famous city of Santa Fé at a little distance looks like an immense brick yard and some of the kilns white washed. The streets (if they be so called) are narrow and dirty in the extreme. The inhabitants (with few exceptions) are about equal to our frontier Indians in all things save courage: they are the greatest cowards on earth! One thousand American riflemen could have defended the pass between this place and St. Mc Gill [San Miguel del Bado, southeast of Santa Fe] (a distance of fifty miles) against the world in arms.

I have been very lucky in procuring quarters being a special friend of *Gov. Bent's*!!! And having been ordered by Gen[l] Kearny to take "military command of New Mexico" when the two Cols. left. I am quartered in Gov. [Manuel] Armijo's palace next to the Gov. A parlor 60 feet in length—4 bedrooms—half a doz. kitchens and store rooms besides a large stable and yard for my gallant old gray. You ought to see my old gray on parade: I always told you he was the greatest horse in the world! But still I dislike paying $10 [pr] bushel for corn to feed him: it is only officers of considerable rank that can get it at that price. The horses and cattle have been mostly sent out to graze—hundreds are dying daily—and the first snow storm will kill 9/10ths of the public stock.

Tell Mr Taylor that Clay weighs 194 lbs. and has a beard and mustach that excites the envy of the Mexican men and the admiration of the women. Walker is looking remarkably well, and makes a first rate drill officer. He is carrying on a little flirtation with the widow Charvis [Barbara Armijo] (the wife of the trader who was murdered).[6] She is very pretty and worth half a million of dollars! Tell Mrs. Taylor to look out for her in the summer. It is near sundown, so I must go on parade and bid you adieu: give my kindest regards to all kin and acquaintances, and above all take care of Chin! Write me a long letter and beg all my friends to do the same—I am lonesome and low spirited. A report reached here this morning that Genl Kearny had been killed by his servant—no one attaches much importance to the rumor, tho' it may be so.[7]

I have written nine pages to Martha [his wife] which I suppose she will show to you all, and which will in a great measure supercede the necessity of writing to each individually.

Ever Yours

D.D. Mitchell

P.S. Three Americans were murdered last night and about 30 Mexicans are taken up on suspicion. Such occurences are quite common. They generally grow out brawls at grog shops and women are generally the cause. We complain of dust in St. Louis. You ought to see Santa Fé! There has not been a drop of rain at the place for seven months.

Martha Berry wrote D. D. Mitchell the following letter.

Martha Mitchell to Lt. Col. David Dawson Mitchell.[8]

Saint Louis, January 29, 1847

How long, how very [long] will it be my beloved husband before I see you again. Alas indeed [as] time passes swiftly with you, the many moments with me, that seem atmost insuportable, and often days & weeks, dull and heavy, were it not for so much quiet happiness & contentment I have in anticipation on your return it would be beyond endurance, but let us hope for the better, is sometimes my motto, when all reflection is banished for otherwise, my heart sinks within me & defies all cheering consolation or hope. We were all at a party given at Grand Ma's by cousin Virginia last night, at which I would not have gone, having been sick several days previous but was over persuaded by Eliza deeming it a duty (as she thought) for us all to go, but I assure you my beloved husband, I feel sensibly the bad effects of my discipation for I am gloomy melancholy (using your own expression) decidedly sick. I know of no other alternative but dosing myself thoroughly for the next week. You cannot conceive what a sacrifice[,] what a violence I have done my feelings by adhereing so strictly to your wishes in not taking polka lessons this winter, for I assure you it is all the go, even Mrs. G—Clarke whom you know [as a] strict member of the church is taking. Oh! indeed my dear husband you have no conception of the mortification I have done both my body & soul which will feign [fain] take you many years of unwearied devotion to repay.

My dear little children I think are improving both in health & appearence.[9] Fanny & Mamy [Mary?] are both exceedingly large for their age, but poor little Sunny [Susan?] instead of increasing she actually decreases in height & width, but her dear little eyes grow larger & so full of mischief she seems to have a perfect recollection of her papa, says he is bad, has gone to Fla. & I must whoop him. I am sure my dear husband if you could only see her you would love her more than ever.

Tell Leo I saw Miss See. Shortly ago she looked [emaciated?] to a perfect skilliton [skeleton] and although she has received a very splendid diamond ring & the world has gone so far as to say she is engaged to Dr. Flemming. I can't but think she has a lurking feeling for him, judging from her apparent emotions, when his name is mentioned but tell him at the same time she is perfectly acquainted of his correspondence with Miss Hempstead.

I never have seen or heard of as much gaity in St. Louis in my life, balls partys, masquerades, concerts, indeed I do not believe there is a night but there is some amusement going on, all of which I am almost entirely exempt from participating, being in the country where they are all such perfect home

bodies, I have but little or no inducement to go. I think you gentlemen will know how to appreciate our sex I should think by
the time you get back, having as I am told by Mr. Simpson such
rare specimens in Sante Fee. Tell Mr. Clarke I feel flattered by
the compliment he paid me in his letter to Mr. Churchill but my
dear husband let me insist that you shall not provoke another
by the same cause, for I think a wife's letter at least should be
held sacred. I desire it should be so as far as mine are concerned
my beloved husband. Give my very best love to Clay, Leo, Mr.
Clarke and my best respects Mr. Waitman [Weightman], Mr.
Jenkins.[10] Also tell them I enjoyn them all to take most excellent
care of you and now my beloved husband having determined to
take a large dose of medicine I must bid you a fond adieu hoping
that when I write again I shall feel in better health & spirits.

Yours forever devoted
Martha

Appendix B

Gertrudis Barceló greatly admired intelligent men. The following was written by her last lover, the Prussian American soldier named August de Marle, who came to Santa Fe in 1846. It was said that de Marle was the most intelligent American ever to come to Santa Fe. From the following excerpt written by him a year and a half before his arrival in the Southwest we are able to glimpse his intellect and passion for public education.

Rom
Translated from French by August de Marle, Leipzig, 1845. Published by Otto Wigand. Copy courtesy of Sven Bivour, Leipzig, Germany. English translation by Harold Kastner, Santa Fe, New Mexico, 1997. In his preface to *Rom* (Rome), de Marle wrote:

Preface of the Translator
I was born to Catholic parents and raised conscientiously in their

faith. I say this only for this reason in advance, because some of my valued coreligionists consider work, which only attack the lie and ignorance of our ancestors, as hateful attacks emanating from protestantism.

I am a Catholic and request that you consider the following sheets worthy of a perusal. Only my love for the truth causes me to contribute to the dissemination of this brochure which has been accepted with great acclaim in Belgium and France but less widely known in Germany until now.

The time has arrived when silence of the educated becomes a crime. Because only ignorance is the cause of all evils of humanity and only poverty prevents most people to inform themselves adequately.

If all were capable to comprehend that only truth, moderation, action, and love alone can really cause happiness, their entire humanity would act only virtuously, and earth would be a paradise.

However, the harshest, of all historic basis devoid of ideas, already inoculated in childhood, make people face each other with hostility. Only now it becomes evident to us that the art of printing is the greatest event from time immemorial; because only now is it becoming possible to communicate with all educated contemporaries in a very short time.

For millennia, and this is a very long time, humanity squirms like a worm under a heavy rock under the still heavy pressure of ignorance and lies, stretching all fibers to realize the urge for harmony and peace innate in all beings in order to be happy; but unfortunately fruitless, because without self confidence, i.e., without development of the human spirit there is no harmony with the all, without true education there is no true happiness.

Oh, could I call to all governments: set up free schools, educate everyone, give freedom to think and to teach, and you erect a golden monument for later times.

This call resounds already for a long time through Germany's provinces and—thank God!—many have listened, and the number of aroused increases every hour. Woe to the cowardly indifference which in most disgraceful materialism at magnificent feasts or luxurious cushions caresses away its existence, while millions eat their bread only with tears, and restlessly in lonely nights on hard straw in vain ring their hands for light and help! Oh, the poor!

It will and must change and the sunshine of truth, the dawn of which the thinkers of our century see already, will rise gloriously above subsequent generations, to fill with happiness those who walk this earth as the eternally inextinguishable light in the sky.

      Leipzig, Feb. 6, 1845   August de Marle

Appendix C

The following is from *Gertrudis Barceló v. G. W. Coulter*, Santa Fe District Court Cases Nos. 241 and 383.

> Mr. [W.] Raymond, a witness on behalf of defendant being called was objected to on ground of interest, objection overruled, duly sworn says, George W. Coulter confessed to have borrowed of G. Barcelo five hundred dollars; witness asked August de Marle who was accustomed to deal monte in company with plaintiff to come to his Tavern—the United States Hotel—to deal monte; de Marle said plaintiff [Tules] would not deal monte in that house while Coulter continued to owe her that debt—the $500—I pro- posed to de Marle that if he would come & deal I would pay him for her $250 in cash, if he would take out the balance $250 in table rent. This he agreed to. I then paid him about $200 & a few days after the balance of the $250, less the deduction for franks [francs] the number of which I do not know or remember. The

day after I paid him the $200 they commence dealing monte in U.S. Hotel—and continued to do so until a man, by the name More, grew violent discharged a pistol over the table & near the person of Mr. De Marle, and broke up the game because as I believe they refused to lend him money—after that time they did not return to play.[1] They had been playing more than eight days in the house. Plaintiff never asked me to pay him $250 nor did he claim any balance due him on the contract I made with him as agent of Madam Barcelo. The charges against plaintiff on the books of Raymond & Coulter for the time they had been playing amounted to about forty seven dollars—plaintiff has never paid said charges. When More committed his act of outrage Madam Barcelo was much scared; I immediately went for the ground and used all diligence to protect Mdm B—against violence—We kept as orderly a house as we could—I remained in partnership with Coulter for some months after this difficulty & have been prepared at all times to comply with the arrangement I made with plaintiff—I had not obligation to pay Coulter's debt and only proposed the arrangement to de Marle to get plff. [Tules] to game at my hotel—My arrangement with de Marle was I think in December 1849—The sum of $47 spoken of above includes the table rent of $5 per night while plff. played. Coulter is in California.

August de Marle being called a second time by plaintiff testified as follows—In September 1848 plaintiff loaned defent $500 for one month without interest if paid in that time, which he failed to pay when due. Mr. Raymond after became a partner of G.C. [George Coulter] & then talked to me several times about going to play at his house, which I refused to do till Coulter paid his debt to plaintiff. Mr. Raymond then proposed if I & plaintiff would game in his house he would pay down $250 & the balance in $250 in eight days—of the $250 paid down 150 were paid in franks as dollars, but which Mr. R—said he would make good—further said that he would furnish us a table free of charge until the balance $250 was paid—We played there more than eight days after our agreement—At that time, the attachment action was pending against Coulter for $500—This is the same action. In the trial of the case in Santa Fe Raymond's book showed charges against plaintiff for about $47—I made no objection to its being deducted from the amount of the debt tho I thot it very high—From the time that More discharged the pistol against me we did not return to play—Raymond went bail for More before the Alcalde (when Moore was arrested for the above offence) which so offended plaintiff that she refused to play again in the house because [Coulter] failed to pay the money in eight days & did not keep such a house as she expected. I so told Raymond—More remained at the Hotel for several months—I asked Raymond for $250 balance of our agreement—I was agent for plaintiff & acted as such in making agreement with Raymond.

The witness further stated that as Colter failed to pay according to original agreement that plaintiff now claimed interest on the money loaned from date. . . .

The Jury then returned a verdict for plaintiff for two hundred fifty seven dollars—

Defendant then moved the court to grant a new trial for the following reasons—which the court overruled.[1]

Notes

Note to Preface

1. In 1851 the new vicar apostolic first arrived in Santa Fe by way of New Orleans, San Antonio, and El Paso from the south on El Camino Real rather than on the Santa Fe Trail from the east.
2. Horgan, *Lamy*, 19.
3. Gregg, *Commerce of the Prairies*, 179.
4. Ruxton, *Ruxton of the Rockies*, 129. Zubiría visited New Mexico in 1833, 1845, and 1850.
5. *Missouri Daily Republican* (MDR), Mar. 27, 1852. Born to Juan Rafael Ortíz and his first wife María Loreta Baca, Juan Felipe Ortíz was baptized Sept. 15, 1797. He became a priest and vicar of Santa Fe under Mexican bishop Zubiría. In opposition to Jean Baptiste Lamy and as a conspirator against the Americans in Dec. 1846, Ortíz left Santa Fe for Durango, Mexico, but later returned, dying of apoplexy on Jan. 20, 1858. Olmsted, "The Ortiz Family of New Mexico," typescript, New Mexico State Archives (NMSA). Don Demetrio Pérez wrote that Ortíz offered Lamy his carriage for the trip to Durango. His account differs from others regarding the number of people and the mode of transportation. Pérez, "New Notes on Bishop Lamy's First Years in New Mexico," *El Palacio* 65:31, 31n7.

6. Horgan, *Lamy*, 175. "Secular" meaning "diocesan," not "regular" trained priest living by the rule of some order or congregation of men such as Franciscans or Benedictines. In 1843 Luján was one of five priests chosen as electors to name the first departmental assembly. Twitchell, *Old Santa Fe*, 231n468. Rafael Chacón mentioned a Father Luján from Mora as a "good friend." Meketa, *Legacy of Honor*, 315.

7. U.S. Census 1860, Santa Fe County. A son, José Esquipulas Luján, was born May 28, 1838, to Father José de Jesús Luján and María Ildefonso Ortíz, paternal grandparents being Francisco Luján and María Magdalena Roibal. Pojoaque Baptisms, Archives of the Archdiocese of Santa Fe (AASF), roll 8, frame 37 (hereafter, the first number following AASF is the microfilm roll, followed by the frame number). The father of Padre Luján, also named José de Jesús, was born March 3, 1786, to Francisco Luján and María Magdalena Roibal. Pojoaque Baptisms, AASF, 8:219–20. The place and birth date for priest José de Jesús Luján is yet to be found (ca.1812?). The U.S. Census for Santa Fe in 1850 lists José de Jesús Luján and Josefa Sánchez y Alarid, ages thirty-eight and thirty-six years, respectively, living in the same household. Father Luján retired to Laguna Salada in Mora County (near Guadalupita), N.Mex., and died Mar. 17, 1885. Vigil, "Mis Tiempos," *La Herencia* 36:41; Mora Burials, AASF, 57:802.

8. Secretary of State Coll., Laws of New Mexico, 1878, NMSA.

9. Horgan, *Lamy*, 175.

10. Ibid., 128.

11. Known to be a heavy drinker, Gov. James Calhoun died of cirrhosis of the liver and/or cholera the following summer of 1852 on the Santa Fe Trail en route to Georgia. He was hastily buried on the waterfront of the Town of Kansas (Kansas City, Mo.) and forgotten for the next 150 years. Cook, "Governor James Silas Calhoun Remembered," *Wagon Tracks* 8:7–8.

12. Horgan, *Lamy*, 115.

13. Ibid., 21; Lempdes Baptisms 1814, Archives of Puy-de-Dôme (APD); Horgan, *Lamy*, 16. Jean Baptiste Lamy was born at 8:00 AM on Oct. 11, 1814, county of Pont-du-Château, to Jean Lamy and Marie Dié. His twin brother, Antoine, died Jan. 1, 1816. Courtesy of Dr. Jean-Pierre Marliac and Michel Allaeys of Aigueperse, Puy-de-Dôme, France; Bernadette Buisson, Bibliothéque de Lempdes, Lempdes, France.

14. Loose Documents 1850–51, AASF, 56:171.

Notes to Chapter 1

1. Sisneros and Torres, *Nombres*, 20. Author Francisco Sisneros is related to Gertrudis Barceló on both his maternal and paternal sides. The Río Bavispe was also known as the Grande, the San Antonio, or the Hiaqui [Yaqui]. Thomas, *Teodoro de Croix and the Northern Frontier of New Spain, 1776–1783*, 162.

2. If a young girl misbehaved she was told, "You are acting like your Tía Barcelona." Interview with Kate Torres Baca, great-granddaughter of María de la Luz Barceló, Feb. 11, 1989, Socorro, N.Mex. Kate was born Mar. 26, 1914, in Musteño, N.Mex., near the Manzano Mountains. Interview with Petra Giddings Riddle, 1994. William Baxter Giddings, father of Petra, erroneously believed Gertrudis Barceló had been born in Barcelona, Spain, rather than in Sonora.

3. See González, *Refusing the Favor*, 59, regarding "La" placed before nicknames or diminutives of women. In 1883 the nomadic Apache diet included the roasted, starchy tule bulb. Bourke, *An Apache Campaign in the Sierra Madre*, 47.

4. A search of the parish poll, ca.1803, for Oposura (Moctezuma) found in the Archivo de la Mitra de Sonora reveals the names of two Barcelonas, Julian and Vizente. Guide to the Parish Archives of Sonora and Sinaloa, film 811, roll 3, UA. Each area is subdivided into three groups: *Españoles* (Spaniards); *Indios del pueblo* (Indians of the town); and *Mestizos* (persons of mixed Indian and Spanish blood), *Indios Laborios* (Indians who worked the agricultural fields on a seasonal basis), *y otras castas* (persons of mixed parentage).

5. Trinidad Barceló to D. Victor Baca, Huasavas, 31 Oct. 1853, in *Manuel Olona v. Victor Baca*, Doña Ana District Civil Court Case, 1854, NMSA.

6. The specific area of Sonora might have eluded researchers had Trinidad not written a return address. I immediately traveled to Sonora to begin the Barceló search and to meet any surviving members of the early Sonoran family. A street in Granados, Sonora, is named Barceló.

7. Interviews in Sonora with Don Tomás Barceló and his son, Agustín Barceló, Moctezuma; Don Francisco Durazo Moreno, Huásabas; and Jorge Provincio Barceló, Granados, May 4–5, 1986. Mention of the Moreno-Barceló family history may be found in "Datos Biográficos de don Venancio Durazo Moreno," typescript, n.d., CC. The Morenos, who intermarried with the Barcelós, date from the seventeenth century in the Huásabas, Sonora, area. In addition, the names of Trinidad and Dolores Barceló, brother and sister-in-law of Tules, appeared as parents in the baptism records for the Nuestra Señora del Rosario Parish, Moctezuma, Sonora, LDS, Batch K600343, Serial Sheet 0391; *Enciclopedia Salvat, Diccionario*, Tomo 2. The name of Sebastián Barceló, a surgeon, appeared in Chihuahua in 1793. Archivos del Ayuntamiento de Chihuahua, ca. 1712–1813, DA. Sargento Manuel Barceló, Cadete Miguel Barceló, and Capt. Simón Barceló served in *milicias* of Trinidad, Yucatán, and the provincia de Cumana prior to 1800. Archivo de Simancas, Hojas de Servicios de América, Secretaria de Guerra (Siglo XVIII), Catalogo XXII, 32.

8. West, *Sonora*, 70–72.

9. Ibid., 76–77.

10. Ibid., 5–6.
11. Calderón de la Barca, *Life in Mexico*, 156.
12. Voss, *On the Periphery of Nineteenth-Century Mexico*, xiii.
13. Sánchez, *Spanish Bluecoats*, 141–44, 175n5 and n7. The Barceló name does not appear in Juan Puyol's list of colonists in 1778. According to Don Tomás Barceló of Moctezuma, Sonora, two Barceló brothers came from Spain to Cuba in the eighteenth century, and after reaching Havana each went his separate way. One brother traveled to northern Mexico and the other to Puerto Rico. This explanation lends credence perhaps to the Barceló's arrival in Sonora with the Domingo Elizondo Expedition of 1767. Sonoran Barcelós also claim that former Puerto Rican president Carlos Romero Barceló is related. Born in 1932 with later degrees from Yale University and the University of Puerto Rico, Carlos Romero Barceló was formerly the mayor of San Juan Puerto, governor of Puerto Rico, and the first Hispanic president of National League of Cities.
14. West, *Sonora*, 44. Trinidad, general superintendent of education at Santa Cruz, N.Mex., sent a set of Ten Regulations on Education to Taos which were endorsed by the village council on Dec. 2, 1827. Loose Documents 1827, AASF, 54:883–88. Territorial Secretary W. G. Ritch described Tules as "a woman of no education but great natural ability." Ritch Coll., roll 1, n.f.
15. In 1764 Jesuit Father Juan Nentvig reconstructed the Huásabas church. Nentvig, *Rudo Ensayo*, 87.
16. Pfefferkorn, *Sonora*, 237. Pfefferkorn used the spelling of Guaisabas.
17. "Datos Biograficos de don Venancio Durazo Moreno," typescript, CC; Leyva, "Vignette of Huasabas, Sonora," *Cochise Quarterly* 20:9–13.
18. Northrop, *Spanish-Mexican Families of Early California: 1769–1850*, 211. I am grateful to Dr. Joseph Sánchez of the Spanish Research Center, University of New Mexico, for calling this source to my attention. On visiting Mission San Francisco Asís (Mission Dolores) in 1990, the author found no grave for María del Pilar León (d. 1808) in the cemetery. She may have been buried in a common grave marked by the Lourdes shrine on the consolidation of the cemetery to its present size. Moraga is buried within the Mission walls. Mission Dolores Brochure, n.d.
19. Nentvig, *Rudo Ensayo*, 3.
20. Voss, *On the Periphery of Nineteenth-Century Mexico*, 73n35. In 1835 instruction in Sonoran primary schools included the *doctrina* (Roman Catholic catechism) and *nocinoes* [sic] *del catecismo político* (civics). In 1803 education in the frontier presidios of Sonora by the chaplains was in accord with instructions from Com. Gen. Nemesio Salcedo (Royal Cedual, 24 Sept. 1803). Children were instructed on Sundays and religious holidays to obey their fathers, "natural and political." On Saturdays family heads sent their "children, servants and slaves" to learn Christian doctrine, according to Fr. Francisco, Obispo de Sonora, Culiacán, Aug. 4,

1803. See "Guide to Parish Archives of Sonora and Sinaloa," film 811, roll 3, fr. 21, UA. In New Mexico, Padre Antonio José Martínez was running a boys' and girls' school by about 1827.

21. Bloom, "New Mexico under Mexican Administration, 1822–1846, Part III," *Old Santa Fe* 1:273n262.

22. The ability to discern counterfeit money, circulating for "some years" in 1824, was critical to any gambler. Bloom, "New Mexico Under Mexican Administration," *Old Santa Fe* (Jan. 1914), 1:239n172.

23. Bandelier, *The Southwestern Journals of Adolph F. Bandelier 1883–1884*, 266. Barceló descendants in Sonora remain cattlemen today. The different cattle brands are listed for the Barceló name by the Departamento de Ganadería, Estado de Sonora. Salcido, *Marcas y Señales para Ganado*, 1963.

24. Barry, *Beginning of the West*, 475.

25. Calderón de la Barca, *Life in Mexico*, 354.

26. Salcido, *Marcas y Señales*, 546.

27. The Jornada del Muerto from Mexico City was the well-traveled route from El Paso taken by clerics and lay alike. Torrez, "Governor Allende's Instructions for Conducting Caravans on the Camino Real, 1816," in *El Camino Real de Tierra Adentro*, 112.

Notes to Chapter 2

1. The *Melgares Report* states that "all kinds of cultivation in Sonora" were grossly neglected. Thomas, "An Anonymous Description of New Mexico, 1818," SHQ 33:60.

2. Bloom, "New Mexico under Mexican Administration," *Old Santa Fe* 1:14–15, 30.

3. Pike, *Journals of Zebulon Montgomery Pike*, 1:406. During early Mar. 1807 Zebulon Pike traveled southward down the Camino Real to Fray Cristóbal, passing through the villages of Peralta, San Fernandez, Tomé (named for Tomé Dominguez), La Joyita, and La Joya de Sevilleta, the principal gathering point for caravans in 1816. North of today's Socorro, Sevilleta was located on the east bank of the Río Grande.

4. The summit of Pikes Peak, called "James's Peak" by Major Stephen H. Long, was ascended on July 14, 1820, by members of Long's expedition. Barry, *Beginning of the West*, 90.

5. Pike, *Journals*, 1:405–6.

6. The population of Santa Fe in the 1850 U.S. census was 4,320. Zebulon Montgomery Pike and his men were subsequently released in Chihuahua. Pike later became a brigadier general and was killed during the War of 1812. His tour through the Southwest in 1806–7 may have been one of exploration and espionage, although it has never been proven. Moorhead, *New Mexico's Royal Road*, 58n7. Maj. Henry Lane Kendrick wrote from

Pueblo, Mex., that the beautiful women of Jalapa wore no drawers—
"oh horrid, to think of *that*." Kendrick, Jan. 13, 1848, Puebla, Mexico,
Misc. mss., New York Historical Society (NYHS).

7. Bancroft, *Arizona and New Mexico*, 17:300.

8. The hacienda may have been Los Ojuelos (meaning "the springs") on the
western slope of the Manzanos. See Simmons, *Little Lion of the Southwest*,
147–54.

9. Tomé Baptisms, AASF, 24:120, 213. The name of Herrero also appears at
various times as Herreros and Herrera. The term *compadrazgo* is a spiritual affinity, or connection contracted by a godfather with the parents of a
child for which he stands sponsor.

10. The Tomé Land Grant, containing approximately 122,000 acres and possessed by descendants of the original 1739 settlers until sold in the late
twentieth century, is one of the last Spanish land grants. The Tajique,
Torreon, Chililí, and Manzano grants were authorized between 1830 and
1840. Espinosa and Chávez, *El Río Abajo*, 92.

11. María Dolores Herrero remarried in Sept. 1823, when she was noted as
the widow of Don Juan Ignacio Barceló. Chávez, *Roots*, 11:1500.

12. Espinosa and Chavez, *El Río Abajo*, 92–93.

13. Chávez, *Origins of New Mexico Families*, 289.

14. San Juan Baptisms, AASF, 9:1171. Manuel Antonio was baptized on Feb. 5,
1802, at age five days. The spellings of surnames such as Chaves/Chávez,
Cisneros/Sisneros, and Gutierres/Gutiérrez vary with the time period.

15. Tomé Marriages, AASF, 33:920. Hermenegildo Cisneros died in 1809 at
Taos Pueblo. Sisneros, "Paternal Line Genealogy of Francisco Sisneros,"
Herencia (1995), 17–20.

16. Lecompte, "The Independent Women of Hispanic New Mexico, 1821–
1846," WHQ 12:18–21; Gregg, *Commerce of the Prairies*, 154.

17. Tomé Marriages, AASF, 33:920. See Chávez, *Roots*, 10:82 (June 20, 1823).

18. Tomé Baptisms, AASF, 24:312, 346; Tomé Burials, AASF, 43:1018, 1030.

19. Baca, "Analysis of Deaths in New Mexico's Río Abajo During the Late
Spanish Colonial and Mexican Periods, 1783–1846," NMHR 70:237–55. See
also Baca, "Infectious Diseases and Smallpox Politics in New Mexico's Río
Abajo, 1847–1920," NMHR 75:107–8.

20. Tomé Baptisms, AASF, 24:368. The entry is signed by Father Francisco
Ignacio de Madariaga with Manuel Sisneros and Gertrudis Barceló acting
as godparents.

21. Santa Fe Marriages, AASF, 31:844. Refugio is recorded as the "adopted
daughter of Dn Manuel Sisneros and Da Gertrudis Barcelón." The honor-
ific title of doña appears first in church records and later, elsewhere.

22. Francisco Ignacio de Madariaga y Serrano became the Tomé parish priest
on July 6, 1821. He died Nov. 17, 1838. Chávez, "Notes and Documents,"
NMHR 31:72.

23. Born in 1480, Cayetano, the cofounder of the Theatine Order, was canonized in 1671.

24. Milford, "Real de Dolores," 1, CC.

25. Piloncillo, the crust of sugar that remains in the boiler.

26. Chacón, *Legacy of Honor*, 70. The early gold mines were known as the Old and New Placers. Placer mining consisted of the rotation of sand and gravel with water (if available) in a wooden *batea* whereby gold settled to the bottom.

27. Milford, "Real de Dolores," 1–2, CC.

28. Ibid., 72, CC. *Cuandos* and *décimas* were extemporaneous poetic compositions in New Mexico about notable people and events of the time. I believe that one or perhaps several were sung about the famous woman gambler named Doña Tules; however, none has yet been found. Rafael Chacón's father, Albino Chacón, was constitutional mayor and judge of the first instance in 1846, serving as the authorizer of miners' claims.

29. Gregg, *Commerce of the Prairies*, 123; Townley, "El Placer," JOW 10:102–15.

30. Willard, "Tour, or Inland Trade with New Mexico," *Early Western Travels 1748–1846*, 18:325–47; Barry, *Beginning of the West*, 119. Dr. Willard began his journey west from Missouri in 1825, arriving in Santa Fe in 1826, rather than 1827 as noted by author John M. Townley.

31. James Purcell of Kentucky is credited with the discovery in 1802 of gold in today's Colorado.

32. Townley, "El Placer," JOW 10:118–21; Ferguson, *New Mexico*, 240.

33. Ibid.; Willard, "Tour, or Inland Trade with New Mexico," 18:325–47. In 1825 Willard traveled the Santa Fe Trail with Augustus Storrs and 105 other traders en route to New Mexico. They reached Taos in early July. Barry, *Beginning of the West*, 119. I am grateful to Homer E. Milford of the New Mexico Abandoned Mine Land Bureau for sharing his extensive research on the name and history of Real del Oro or Real de Dolores. In 1832 the name of Real de Dolores apparently became the official name, although various names continued to be used, such as Ojo del Oso or Oro, Real de los Dolores del Oro, El Placer, New Placers, etc. Milford to Cook, Santa Fe, N.Mex., Jan. 23, 1997.

34. Twitchell, *The Leading Facts of New Mexican History*, 2:132.

35. SANM II, 3:814. See also MANM, 29:11.

36. MANM, 29:17, 23, 27.

37. Ibid., 5:1102; Certificate of María Gertrudis Barceló, June 9, 1835, MANM, 20:186.

38. Lecompte, "The Independent Women of Hispanic New Mexico, 1821–1846," WHQ 12:34.

39. Gregg, *Commerce of the Prairies*, 119.

40. Albuquerque attorney Gilberto Espinosa once wrote, sans footnotes, that Juan Ignacio Barceló was a professional card player. "Doña Tules:

The Sharpest Monte Dealer in the Territory," *Century* (n.d.), vertical file, NMSL. For a brief biographical sketch of Gilberto Espinosa see Espinosa and Chávez, *El Río Abajo*, n.p.

41. Gregg, *Commerce of the Prairies*, 168.

42. Elliott, *The Mexican War Correspondence of Richard Smith Elliott*, 165. In nineteenth-century New Mexican handwriting the "r" looks like an "x."

43. Questionable twentieth-century documents and drawings in the Taos archives would lead one to believe this to be true.

44. Rubio, *Refranes, Proverbios y Dichos y Dicharachos Mexicanos*, 1:200.

45. Santa Fe Baptisms, AASF, 16:981. In 1833 Manuel Sisneros and Getrudis [*sic*] Barceló were godparents to José Panfilio Luciano, grandson of José Caballero and Rita Olona.

46. Santa Fe Baptisms, AASF, 16:981, 1065 and 17:188, 787; Santa Fe Baptisms, AASF, 31:170; Santa Fe Marriages, AASF, 31:844, 1107; Santa Fe Burials, AASF, 41:235, 275.

47. Tomé Marriages, AASF, 33:920. In Diligencia 43 Dolores Herrero is recorded as the widow of Don Juan Ignacio Barceló. Chávez, *Roots*, 11:1500. Dolores Herrero de Barceló is inadvertently confused with the wife of her son Trinidad, also named Dolores.

48. The name of Dolores Herrero is found on the Juan Bautista Vigil map of Santa Fe dated Jan. 26, 1836. Manuel Antonio and Doña Tules have four servants. SANM I, 6:1227–29; MANM, 30:349.

49. Sherman, *Santa Fe: A Pictorial History*, 15–16.

50. Santa Fe Burials, AASF, 40:1066. In 1816 Pedro married Ana María Baca and together they have several children, Facundo Pino being the last born on Nov. 17, 1823. Ana María Baca, age 53, appears on the 1841 Santa Fe census. Chávez, *Origins of New Mexico Families*, 259–60.

51. Gregg, *Commerce of the Prairies*, 293–94.

52. Ibid., 294.

53. Milford, "Real de Dolores," 13; Josiah Gregg, *Commerce of the Prairies*, 331n1; Barry, *Beginning of the West*, 430, 475–76.

54. Born in Kentucky on Mar. 26, ca. 1813, James Giddings was the son of George Giddings (b. in Maryland) and Frances Tandy (b. in Virginia). James M. Giddings and Petra Gutierres were married in 1842. Santa Fe Marriages, AASF, 31:868.

55. Barry, *Beginning of the West*, 430.

56. Santiago Flores and Refugio Sisneros were married Aug. 17, 1841. Santa Fe Marriages, AASF, 31:844. Born ca. 1820 in Chihuahua, Flores was the son of Don Ignacio Flores and Lucía Molina.

57. Santa Fe Baptisms, AASF, 17:188, 287, 577; Index for the Parish of El Sagrario, Chihuahua, Mexico, LDS.

58. Boyle, *Comerciantes, Arrieros, y Peones*, 44, 142.

59. Ibid., 44, 142.

NOTES TO PAGES 21–26

60. In Apr. 1843 New Mexico trader Antonio José Chávez was murdered and robbed of thirty-nine gold doubloons in his money belt and $3,000 in gold dust on the Santa Fe Trail. See Simmons, *Murder on the Santa Fe Trail, An International Incident, 1843*, 29, 32.

61. Monterde's full title was J. Mariano Monterde, General Graduado de Brigada, Gobernador y Commandante General del Departamento de Chihuahua. *Revista Oficial*, 27 Diciembre de 1842.

62. Cook, "Gertrudis Barceló, Woman Entrepreneur of the Chihuahua and Santa Fe Trails, 1830–1850," *El Camino Real de Tierra Adentro*, 2:242. Regarding the Armijo-Barceló partnership see p. 38.

63. Barry, *Beginning of the West*, 571.

64. MDR, Mar. 26, 1846.

65. Barry, *Beginning of the West*, 580.

66. See Josiah Gregg, *Commerce of the Prairies*, 332, for a statistical table of probable amounts from 1822 to 1843, with revisions, of merchandise, wagons, men, and proprietors engaged in the Santa Fe and Chihuahua trade. Estimated Dolores gold production from 1822 to 1843 indicates a cumulative total of $754,400 in gold and $2,922,000 in merchandise (taken from Gregg). Milford, "Real de Dolores, Nomination for the Mining History Association's Year of Mining and Historic Preservation, 1999," CC.

67. Woodruff, "Doniphan's Expedition—War with Mexico, 1846," *Missouri Miscellany*, 11:18.

68. *Die Tägliche Deutsche Tribüne*, Aug. 21, 1847. No documents concerning mine ownership by Gertrudis Barceló could be found.

69. Ibid., Dec. 10, 1847. Courtesy Gerd Alfred Petermann. No church records show a marriage between Gertrudis Barceló and August de Marle, also a Catholic.

Notes to Chapter 3

1. Gregg, *Commerce of the Prairies*, 168. See a list of friars who gambled in 1817. SANM II, 18:863.

2. Punter: one who plays against the bank.

3. Untitled typescript from Bent's Old Fort, courtesy Charles Bennett, Palace of the Governors.

4. Richardson, *Beyond the Mississippi*, 251; Diary of Philip Gooch Ferguson, MHS.

5. TANM, 45: 774. Dram shop: a saloon.

6. Judicial Proceedings, MANM, 20:186.

7. Letter to editor, NYDTi, Dec. 17, 1892. On the death of Doña Tules in 1852, August de Marle was appointed an executor of her estate.

8. Allison, "Santa Fe in 1846," *Old Santa Fe* 2:402; Richardson, *Beyond the Mississippi*, 251.

9. SFNM, May 8, 1913.

10. Sunder, *Matt Field on the Santa Fe Trail*, 208.

11. Ibid., 208.

12. Jeremy Francis Gilmer Papers, Lenoir Family Papers, No. 2, Nov. 6, 1846, UNC.

13. *Manuel Alvarez v. James Giddings et al.* (1850), U.S. District Court Records, Santa Fe County Case File #230.

14. While serving in the early 1840s as U.S. consul in Santa Fe, Manuel Alvarez retained his Mexican citizenship despite never fulfilling the requirements for U.S. citizenship. He may have retained his Spanish citizenship as well. Chávez, *Manuel Alvarez 1794–1856: A Southwestern Biography*, 39–41. The suspicious Doña Tules, a patron of Alvarez, possessed the ability to recognize his arrogant personality.

15. Read Coll. I, NMSA, reverse of #256, noted in handwriting of Alvarez.

16. Sunder, *Matt Field on the Santa Fe Trail*, 209.

17. Brewerton, "Incidents of Travel in New Mexico," *Harper's*, 588.

18. Sunder, *Matt Field on the Santa Fe Trail*, 208.

19. Ibid., 212.

20. Dunlap, "Journal of Dr. J. N. Dunlap, Santa Fe 1847 [1846]," 4, NMSA.

21. Sunder, *Matt Field on the Santa Fe Trail*, 212.

22. Ibid., 212.

23. SFWG, Nov. 15, 1856; Gregg, *Commerce of the Prairies*, 169; Rubenstein, "Chuza: A New Mexico Gambling Wheel," typescript, ACHLA. Chusa was a precursor to the roulette wheel.

24. Diary of Philip Gooch Ferguson, MHS.

25. Rickey, *Forty Miles a Day on Beans and Hay*, 126, 208; Cleland, *This Reckless Breed of Men*, 148; Chacón, *Legacy of Honor*, 17. See Marqués de la Nava de Brazinas (Vargas), *bando* of 1703 prohibiting gambling by soldiers. SANM II, 3:814.

26. Bieber, *Journal of a Soldier under Kearny and Doniphan*, 268.

27. Owens receipt, Santa Fe Papers 1830–58, MHS. Josiah Gregg lists the following Mexican money table: 12 *granos* equal 1 real; 8 reales, 1 peso or dollar. The par value of the doubloon or gold coin was sixteen dollars. Gregg, *Commerce of the Prairies*, 298n6. See also Kaye, "Specie on the Santa Fe Trail," *Wagon Tracks* 14:10; Simmons, "New Mexico's Money Crunch," Apr. 15–21, 1998, SFR.

28. *The Gamblers*, 85.

29. SFWG, Feb. 18, 1854. In 1843 Carlos Beaubien was a partner with Guadalupe Miranda in the large Maxwell Land Grant, which encompassed northeastern New Mexico into southern Colorado.

30. Huning, *Trader on the Santa Fe Trail, Memoirs of Franz Huning*, 21–23; Twitchell, *Old Santa Fe*, 340n617; SFNM, Jan. 12, 1867. James L. Collins, a native of Crab Orchard, Ky., and later resident of Booneville, Mo., first

came to N.Mex. in 1826 as a trader. Founder and editor of the *Santa Fe Weekly Gazette*, he occupied other offices in the Indian agency and as U.S. depository. SFWG, June 12, 1869. Born Aug. 8, 1823, near Boston, Mass., Charles Lawrence Thayer was robbed and stranded in El Paso in 1849 while en route to the Calif. gold fields. He then traveled to Santa Fe where he remained, freighting on the Santa Fe Trail between Santa Fe and Leavenworth. By 1878 a professional gambler, Thayer married Guadalupe Ortíz and died Feb. 22, 1907. SFNM, Feb. 22, 1907.

31. Santa Fe Papers, 1830–58, MHS. In 1847, merchant Samuel Owens of Independence, Mo., died in battle during the Mexican War.

32. Judicial Proceedings, 1839, MANM 26:623.

33. SFR, Nov. 20, Dec. 25, 1847. Feared by the Apaches, the cunning Santiago Kirker was hired as a guide and interpreter by the U.S. government. See Connelly, *Doniphan's Expedition* and McGaw, *Savage Scene*.

34. Richardson, *Beyond the Mississippi*, 251. Born in St. Louis in 1802, Cerán St. Vrain formed a partnership with Charles and William Bent in 1830 resulting in one of the most profitable trading companies. The wealthy Ceran St. Vrain owned a large and well-known ranch in Cimarron, N.Mex., later moving to Mora where he engaged in politics, land speculation, and flour milling. He died in 1870 and is buried there. Thrapp, *Encyclopedia*, 3:1260; Dunham, "Ceran St. Vrain," in Hafen, *Mountain Men and the Fur Trade*, 5:297–316.

35. Twitchell, *Old Santa Fe*, 340–41.

36. Dunlap, "Journal of Dr. J. N. Dunlap, Santa Fe 1847," NMSA.

37. Santa Fe Baptisms, AASF, 16:981.

38. Meyer, *Mary Donoho*, 8–9. Harriet Donoho, born in 1835, is the earliest known Anglo American child born in Santa Fe.

39. Ibid., 41. Doña Tules was described by Charles Conklin "a very fine and attractive woman, about middle size, very large black [eyes?] and black hair [rather than red], weighing about 140 pounds." She may have used henna on her hair. Chávez Letter, NMSA.

40. This is indeed Dolores, the mother of Tules, rather than Dolores, her sister-in-law. Dolores Griego de Barceló and Trinidad, brother of Tules, were living in "San Fernandes" (near Taos) in Jan. 1832, where they buried their six-month old child. Taos Burials, AASF, 42:181.

41. In various documents Rafaela is also called Sisneros and Barceló; on the 1841 census her name is given as Petrita Rafaela. Santa Fe Burials, AASF, 41:235.

42. SANM I, 6:1227–29.

43. Ballesteros, Benander, and Moline, "History of Settlement and Community: The Barrio del Torreón," 1–6.

44. Gregg, *Commerce of the Prairies*, 168.

45. Sunder, *Matt Field on the Santa Fe Trail*, 209.

46. Lecompte, *Rebellion in Río Arriba*, 9. Manuel Armijo served as New Mexico governor for three terms: 1827–29, 1837–44, and 1845–46. The remote and dictatorial government located in Mexico City caused several rebellions occurring at this time in Tex., Calif., as well as in several Mexican states.

47. Lecompte, *Rebellion in Rio Arriba*, 13.

48. Ibid., 115, 165n50.

49. Ritch Coll., roll 1:n.f., NMSA. Another account credits others with the burial of the head of Gov. Pérez, but Ritch noted that he had interviewed Juana Prada, one of the women with Doña Tules. In the 1841 Santa Fe census Juana Prada lived at #7 in the Barrio del Torreón, age twenty-nine. MANM, 30:350.

50. Rickey, *Forty Miles a Day on Beans and Hay*, 126, 208; Cleland, *This Reckless Breed of Men*, 148; Chacón, *Legacy of Honor*, 17.

51. Gregg, *Commerce of the Prairies*, 168; Elliott, *The Mexican War Correspondence of Richard Smith Elliott*, 165.

52. Brewerton, "Incidents of Travel in New Mexico," *Harper's*, 588.

53. Following a sheep drive to Calif., Henry Cuniffe returned to Santa Fe in 1853 with $70,000 in coin and gold. Whether he applied this profit against the Barceló debt of 1848 remains unknown. Kingsbury, *Trading in Santa Fe*, 7n50.

54. Santa Fe County District Court, Civil Case #241 (Attachment, Oct. 1849), NMSA.

55. A fictional account of this encounter in the United States Hotel may be found in Laughlin, *The Wind Leaves No Shadow*, 343–44.

56. Bennett, *Forts and Forays*, 27.

57. SFWG, Dec. 21, 1867.

58. See Appendix C for details of the Barceló-Coulter trial.

Notes to Chapter 4

1. Alvarez to Buchanan, Sept. 4, 1846, RG 199, CD, NA.

2. Young, *The West of Philip St. George Cooke*, 179; MDR, Jan. 1 and Mar. 19, 1846.

3. Bieber, *Journal of a Soldier under Kearny and Doniphan*, 261; Glasgow and Glasgow, *Brothers on the Santa Fe and Chihuahua Trails*, 91.

4. María de la Luz Barceló, sister of Doña Tules, lived in the village of Tajique in the Manzano area.

5. Alfred S. Waugh wrote, "With this lady his Excellency is very intimate; indeed, I believe, he is a partner in her business." Waugh, *Travels in Search of the Elephant*, 121.

6. Tyler, "Governor Armijo's Moment of Truth," *The Mexican War*, 142.

7. Ibid., 11:313.

8. Unfortunately, as yet there is no authoritative biography of Manuel Armijo.

9. The wheat-colored El Paso wine was strong and sweet.

10. *Niles' National Register*, Nov. 7, 1846.

11. The U.S. Hotel became known as the Exchange and later as La Fonda Hotel.

12. Accts. of Major Thomas Swords, Quartermaster, RG 217, NA. I am grateful to Harry Myers, NPS, for this citation.

13. *St. Louis Weekly Reveille*, Mar. 1, 1847.

14. General Kearny appointed Lucius F. Thruston prefect of Santa Fe County. A Chihuahua merchant for many years, he was known as a professional gambler.

15. Book of Judicial Conciliations (1835), Jusgado 1°, MANM 20:131; Proceedings (1835), Jusgado 2°, MANM 20:460.

16. The house occupied by the Magoffins in 1846 was across San Francisco Street from La Parroquia (parish church), today the parking building area of La Fonda Hotel. The author recalls taking violin lessons in this primitive adobe house in 1940. It had crude, wide-planked flooring, and very low ceilings.

17. Magoffin, *Down the Santa Fe Trail*, 107.

18. *Statement of Buildings Rented by the Quartermaster's Department at the Post of Santa Fe, New Mexico*, in the report of Secretary of War Conrad. 32 Cong., 1st sess., House Exec. Doc. 2, 1851.

19. Elliott, *The Mexican War Correspondence of Richard Smith Elliott*, 211.

20. Ibid.

21. Hall, *Medicine on the Santa Fe Trail*, 118; U.S. Census for San Miguel County in 1850. Twenty-six cases of gonorrhea, fifteen cases of orchitis, and ten cases of primary syphilis were noted in 1847.

22. Magoffin, *Down the Santa Fe Trail*, 120–21. The cuna incorporated a rocking motion. Tules may have purchased her false teeth in Chihuahua; false teeth were patented in 1822.

23. David Dawson Mitchell, a cultured man and successful fur trader with the Ioway Outfit of the Western Department, was born in Louisa County, Virginia, July 31, 1806, and died May 23, 1861, in St. Louis, Mo. According to his obituary, he died at age fifty-five in the Planters' House in St. Louis. *Missouri Republican*, May 24, 1861. Although Mitchell was buried in Calvary Cemetery in St. Louis, apparently his tombstone, along with a thousand others, was demolished by cemetery administrators in 1951. MDR, Aug. 5, 1851. The Calvary Cemetery office today has no record of his burial there. In 1840 Mitchell married Martha Eliza Berry, daughter of Maj. Taylor Berry, retired army officer and entrepreneur. *Dictionary of American Biography*, 13:41. When she died he had her buried in the yard of what was then his downtown house, so he could look from his window

onto her grave. File Cards, MHS. He became U.S. superintendent of Indian Affairs in 1841 and held the position intermittently until 1852.

24. Gibson, *Journal of a Soldier under Kearny and Doniphan*, 246n380; Barry, *Beginning of the West*, 658.

25. Risch, *Quartermaster Support of the Army*, 251. Congress enacted legislation requiring volunteers to furnish their own clothing, granting $3.50 per month.

26. Elliott, *The Mexican War Correspondence of Richard Smith Elliott*, 209–15. See Appendix A for letters written at the time of the Mexican War by D. D. Mitchell to his friend Judge R. Wash, and to Mitchell from his wife. Ladies of St. Louis, Mo., purportedly swooned when they passed the handsome Lt. Col. Mitchell on the street.

27. Ibid., 212.

28. Twitchell, *Old Santa Fe*, 338.

29. Cook, "Pizarro and Doña Tules at the Palace," *Compadres* 3:4–8. *Pizarro* was the first play enacted in English in New Mexico. Dabney and Russell, editors, *Dargon Historical Essays*, 65–76.

30. Elliott, *The Mexican War Correspondence of Richard Smith Elliott*, 214.

31. Ibid., 215, 264n5. During the Civil War, Isleta Pueblo governor Ambrosio Abeita loaned approximately $20,000 to pay U.S. troops in New Mexico. Lummis, *Mesa, Cañon and Pueblo*, 446.

32. Kennerly, *Persimmon Hill*, 192.

33. Glasgow and Glasgow, *Brothers on the Santa Fe and Chihuahua Trails*, 120. Glasgow and other traders continued their trip to Chihuahua in order to sell their wares.

34. No evidence of any repayment was found in the paymaster's records. Oral history of the Barceló family claims "some government men" came during the early twentieth century and gave them a one dollar bill to settle the claim. No proof of this has yet been found.

35. Mattison, "David Dawson Mitchell," in *The Mountain Men and the Fur Trade of the Far West*, 2:242–44. At Fort McKenzie, Karl Bodmer depicted the battle, one of his most famous paintings. Author Ray Mattison recorded the death of Mitchell incorrectly as May 31, rather than May 23, 1861. MDR, May 24, 1861. See also Verdon, "David Dawson Mitchell: Virginian on the Wild Missouri," *Magazine of Montana*, 27:2–15.

36. Mitchell's first known wife, who died of smallpox, was a member of the notorious Assiniboine-half-breed Deschamps family of the Upper Missouri River. The father, François Deschamps, murdered Governor Robert Semple in 1816 during the Red River massacre. Larpenteur, *Forty Years a Fur Trader*, 1:95–97. Assiniboine artist Charles Mitchell, great-great-grandson of D. D. Mitchell, stayed with the author during the Santa Fe Indian Markets of 1996 and 2004. Mary Mitchell (1828–1919), Sac and Fox daughter of Julia Mitchell and David D. Mitchell, was educated at a

Quaker school in Philadelphia and in 1894 married Chief Moses Keokuk, Jr. The author visited the grave of Mary Mitchell near Stroud, Okla. Obit., *Stroud Messinger*, May 6, 1919.

37. Mattison, *The Mountain Men and the Fur Trade of the Far West*, 2:246. D. D. Mitchell married Martha Eliza Berry in 1840 following his tenure on the upper Missouri River.

38. Brayer, *William Blackmore: The Spanish-Mexican Land Grants of New Mexico and Colorado, 1863–1878*, 1:128–29.

39. Colfax County Civil Court Records, Case 768, NMSA; Colfax County District Court, First Judicial District, Bill of Complaint, *Henry Clark and Wife Fannie Clark et al v. Maxwell Land-Grant Company*, Sept. 1889; Colfax County Records, Deed Book B, 210–29. Murphy, "The Beaubien and Miranda Land Grant, 1841–1846," NMHR 42:47. The spurious record indicated that Donaciano Vigil and Ceran St. Vrain, who purportedly acted as "Administrator for Charles Bent, deceased," conveyed the land. However, Bent did not die until Jan. 1847. Despite blatant discrepancies, the document was permitted to stand as a legal conveyance of the interests of Cornelio Vigil, Cerán St. Vrain, and Donaciano Vigil. Bent was a partner of trader-merchant St. Vrain, and Vigil, territorial secretary under Armijo. The original deed appears to be missing. See also Lecompte, "Manuel Armijo and the Americans," 62n41. The agreement deserves further scrutiny.

40. Waugh, *Travels in Search of the Elephant*, 121. See Connelley, *Doniphan's Expedition*, 513; Augustín Durán, according to Prince, *Historical Sketches of New Mexico*, 168n32; Twitchell in his *The Leading Facts of New Mexico History* wrote that Tules herself told Col. Sterling Price. Sterling Price gambled with Tules during 1846 and 1847. A graduate of the U.S. Military Academy, Lt. A. B. Dyer, chief of ordnance, recorded, "Col. P. left early, having won a few dollars." Journal of Alexander Brydie Dyer, ACHLA; "Notes and Documents," NMHR 22:4.

41. The *New Orleans Picayune* carried a series of articles by George Kendall.

42. Benjamin Read Coll. I, reverse of no. 256, NMSA.

43. Journal of Henry Caspers, SLML; Connelley, *Doniphan's Expedition*, 578–80. My thanks to Mark Gardner for the Caspers reference. Tules may have been visiting her younger sister, María de la Luz, or perhaps the gold mines at Real de Dolores.

44. William Ziegler Angney was born Oct. 3, 1818, in Carlisle, Cumberland County, Pa., and died Jan. 28, 1878, in Santa Clara County, Calif. From Pennsylvania, he came to Jefferson City, Mo., where he practiced law. At the outbreak of the Mexican War, Angney came to Santa Fe as a captain in the Cole County volunteers. In a letter dated Jan. 30, 1852, to Manuel Alvarez, Angney sent word to "Madam Tule" that he never had a chance to pursue her debt against [Louis?] Robidoux due to a fire, which burned

his papers in San Francisco. The news arrived too late; Tules had died
some thirteen days earlier. Alvarez Business Papers, 1852, NMSA. While
in Santa Fe in 1849 Angney married Isabel Conklin, who later sued him
for abandonment. Santa Fe Marriages, AASF, 31:1035. His second wife was
Lydia Frances Witham; see Witham, *Garden of the World*, 313–14.
45. SFR, Dec. 4, 1847.
46. Ibid, Dec. 18, 1847.
47. Ibid., Aug. 16, 1848.
48. SANM I, 25:754; SANM I, 28: 757; Boyle, *Comerciantes, Arrieros, y
Peones*, 135; Simmons, "A Problem with Mule Packing Terminology,"
Wagon Tracks 10:7. Simmons gives a tentative explanation of the different categories carried by mules and listed in Spanish documents such as
bultos, tercios, cajones, bailes, and piezas.
49. The Morenos had married into the Sonoran Barceló family. See chapter 1.
50. Simmons, *The Little Lion of the Southwest*, 55–60.
51. Bek, "The Followers of Duden," in Wulfing, "Twelfth Article," *Missouri
Historical Review* 17:598–99.

Notes to Chapter 5
1. Magoffin, *Down the Santa Fe Trail*, 120–21; Sunder, *Matt Field on the
Santa Fe Trail*, 208; Elliott, *The Mexican War Correspondence of Richard
Smith Elliott*, 165; DNM, April 19, 1869. On visiting Santa Fe in 1883,
trader Reuben Gentry recalled the store he and his partner, James M.
Giddings, operated on the south side of the plaza, as well as "the then
popular resort kept by Gertrudes Barceló, where Manuel Armijo . . . ran
a monte bank." According to Gentry's description, this monte bank occu-
pied the general area of the old La Castrense, or military chapel. SFNM,
Oct. 4, 1883. In 1855 Col. John Grayson brought George Carter to Santa
Fe from Zanesville, Ohio, as his "body-servant." DNM, June 14, 1880. The
respected Carter died in 1880 and was buried in the Masonic Cemetery,
under the asphalt parking lot immediately south of the today's Masonic
Lodge west of the pink-colored Scottish Rite Temple. Some of Santa
Fe's most prominent people served as pallbearers: Lehman Spiegelberg,
Joseph Stinson, James L. Johnson, Judge Henry S. Waldo, Col. William
Craig, and Gov. W. F. M. Arny. A territorial deed history of the Exchange
Hotel is found in Kingsbury, *Trading in Santa Fe*, 42n21.
2. Elliott, *The Mexican War Correspondence of Richard Smith Elliott*, 165–66,
257n145, 211–15.
3. Ibid., 165.
4. Sunder, *Matt Field on the Santa Fe Trail*, 208.
5. This site is yet to be documented by deed history. Author Ruth Laughlin,
born and raised in Santa Fe, noted that the southeast corner of Burro

Alley at Palace Ave. was demolished and became an automobile show-room. I recall walking past this showroom many times in the 1940s.

6. Allison, "Santa Fe in 1846," *Old Santa Fe* (April 1915), 402.

7. See chapter 4.

8. Brewerton, "Incidents of Travel in New Mexico," 587. Brewerton's sketches illustrated his articles, which appeared in *Harper's New Monthly Magazine* issues from 1853 to 1862, although not all can be attributed to him.

9. Ibid., 589.

10. A fist-sized bag of nuggets and dust weighed about ten pounds. *The Gamblers*, 85.

11. See Santa Fe County Records, Deed Book B-79, which in 1854 records "[property] described as follows: on the north, by a sandy arroyo, on the South by an old street and the public grounds known as the Muralla." Albert Pike described the center of Santa Fe: "There is the public square [the plaza] surrounded with blocks of mud buildings. . . . Within forty yards of this square there is another called the muralla, surrounded like-wise by buildings. . . . It is used as a wheat field, and belongs to the sol-diers who have their dwellings around it." SFNM, Jan. 27, 1910.

12. Richardson, *Beyond the Mississippi*, 251. See Lieutenant Alexander B. Dyer Journal, 1846–47, ACHLA.

13. Her residence on Grant and Palace Avenues was demolished in 1938–39, the year this writer arrived in Santa Fe. The county courthouse may soon be sold or demolished. The property abutting her residence to the south was demolished when the Lensic Theater opened in 1931. The gambling sala at the corner of Palace and Burro Alley remained until the late 1940s. The fourth building to the east was demolished and became a brick house for the Candelario family. See "City of Santa Fe, New Mexico, Memo," Aug. 19, 1999, 40; Hanks, "Archival Report for Palace-Grant Ave.-Burro Alley Intersection, Santa Fe, New Mexico," April 3, 1995, CC. The name of Burro Alley has changed throughout history: Gertrudis Barcelona Street (1878); Picayune Alley (1880); Taos Place "or as it is usually called Burro Alley" (1883); and Gold Alley (1901). Santa Fe County Records, Lease Book Y: 273; Gold ad in SFNM, Feb. 27, 1880; *New Mexican Review*, Oct. 5, 24, 1883. In 1945 there was a movement to widen Burro Alley and make Grant Avenue a boulevard from Federal Place to the State Capitol, according to A. B. Renehan. SFNM, Aug. 6, 1945. A suggestion was made to widen the streets of Santa Fe and speed up the traffic.

14. SANM I, 1:1106.

15. Lecompte, *Rebellion in Río Arriba*, 138. Tules possibly won a portion of this property in a game of monte.

16. Translation by Roman L. Baca. NMSA. See "City of Santa Fe, New Mexico, Memo," 38–39, Aug. 19, 1999, to Archaeological Review Committee Members from Mary G. Ragins, Historic Preservation

Planner. On p. 49 the report incorrectly gives the location of the gambling sala of Gertrudis Barcelo as the Lensic Sandwich Shop at the corner at Burro Alley and San Francisco Street.

17. Interviews with Tony Mignardot, Feb. 25, 1985, and Ruben (Ruby) Gomez, Sept. 10, 1986, both of whom lived in the Barceló house.

18. Santa Fe County Records, Deed Book B, 102. In 1850 the Gertrudis Barceló residence was bequeathed to her younger sister, María de la Luz, of Valencia County.

19. SFWG, Nov. 13, 1852.

20. Santa Fe County Records, Deed Book B, 104.

21. Davis to Lewis, Sept. 25, 1857, State Dept., Territorial Papers, New Mexico 1851–72, roll T-17, NA; Towne, "Printing in New Mexico," NMHR 35:109; Stratton, *The Territorial Press of New Mexico 1834–1912*, 205.

22. SFWG, June 12, 1869. The body of James L. Collins was moved from the old Masonic Cemetery to the National Cemetery in Santa Fe. For more discussion on the death of Collins, see Meketa, *From Martyrs to Murderers*, 76–86.

23. SFWG, May 22, 1858.

24. Ibid., Feb. 19, 1853; May 15, 1858. At the outset of his purchase of the Doña Tules residence in 1853 a letter to the newspaper editor incorrectly comments that Collins was "fitting it up" for use of the Indian Agency. By 1881 the Collins Building appears in an ad for sale. DNM, Mar. 18, 1881.

25. Santa Fe County Records, Deed Book D, 1. The appreciation may have been the result of the joining of the two houses owned by James L. Collins, who planned to move the Indian Department into his former house which became known as the Collins Building. SFWG, Feb. 19, 1853; DNM, Mar. 18, 1881.

26. Santa Fe County Records, Deed Book N, 103.

27. SFNM, Oct. 9, 1883.

28. Santa Fe County Records, Deed Book N, 626. W. G. Ritch is described as a sedate and dignified character. He left Santa Fe to become the postmaster in Engle, N.Mex., where he insisted that writer-rancher Eugene Manlove Rhodes address him as "governor" before he would give him his mail.

29. Ibid., Deed Book N, 106. Tony Mignardot recalled spending his honeymoon in the Barceló house. Emile and Maria Mignardot, parents of Tony, were from France and claimed to be related to Archbishop Jean-Bapiste Pitaval. SFNM, Feb. 16, 1928, and Jan. 13, 2004.

30. SFNM, Feb. 16, 1928, and June 15, 1958.

31. Ibid., Dec. 9, 1938. Plans are presently in the works in 2006 to build a new courthouse.

32. Historian Ralph Emerson Twitchell in *Old Santa Fe* wrote that "her resort was located on the corner of San Francisco street and Burro alley

and extended through to Palace avenue on the north." However, no deed description has yet been found that extends the Barceló property more than sixty feet from the corner of Burro Alley south to San Francisco Street.

33. Georgetown University graduate A. B. Renehan was an attorney who came to Santa Fe in 1892. From 1898 to 1900 he acted as secretary of the democratic territorial central committee.

34. SFNM, Jan. 18 and 21, 1904.

35. Ibid., July 27 and Sept. 11, 1926. In 1953 the rear became the Shed Restaurant, now in Prince Plaza on East Palace Ave.

36. Ibid., Nov. 23, 1923; Aug. 31 and Sept. 20, 1926. The Smith-McGinnis Motor Co. sold Chrysler cars in July 1926, becoming the Bode-Smith Motor Co. in 1927, defunct by 1928. The Nash car came to Santa Fe in 1929 via the Venner Nash Motor Co. SFNM, Jan. 7, 1929. By 1930–31 the red bricked J. S. Candelario house was built, Montgomery Ward & Co. opened a catalogue office to the immediate west, and Emblem & Sauer Packard Service Station occupied the corner in 1938. Santa Fe City Directory, 1930–31, 1936–37, 1953. By 1953 Frank's Capitol Liquors and Cocktail Lounge occupied the Montgomery-Ward space and Southwestern Publishing Co. opened in the automobile showroom built of hollow tile. Interview with Martin J. Bode, Jr., Feb. 4, 1989. A bronze burro sculpted by Charles Southard in 1988 guards the southern entrance to Burro Alley today.

37. See Santa Fe County Records, Deed Book L, 94, and Y, 194–95. I am grateful to Richard Montoya for access to the deed history of the Bokum Building.

38. Richard D. Bokum acquired the Candelario property prior to building the Palace Restaurant. Bokum to Cook, Jan. 24, 1989. The addition called Bokum Plaza was planned in 1955 by Bokum and Judge Harry L. Bigbee.

39. SFNM, Apr. 12, 1959.

40. Santa Fe County Records, Deed Book D, 537; Santa Fe County Records, Deed Book Y, 273; *New Mexican*, Oct. 5, 1883, May 24, 1955.

41. The author attended a Spanish class taught by Marie Isabel Sena in the old Sena building of Santa Fe High School (now demolished), two blocks north of Burro Alley. We hovered under our desks while covering our ears against the deafening sirens.

42. SFNM, Apr. 28, 1930. Parts of these houses were sold at auction.

43. Ibid., Feb. 13, 1990.

44. Ibid., Mar. 5, 1990; Interview with David Gallegos, Dec. 10, 1984. Barber Joe Gonzales also cut the hair of the author's two sons and husband for many years.

45. Ibid., July 27, 1926.

Notes to Chapter 6

1. Secretary of State Coll., Last Wills and Testament Act, Laws of New Mexico, 1852. NMSA.

2. Ibid.

3. See Santa Fe County Probate Records, Probate Case File 1005 no. 87, NMSA. Dashes have been replaced by periods, and commas added for clarity.

4. In 1851 Maj. John Munroe and Lt. Lafayette McLaws rented from Gertrudis Barceló. *Statement of Buildings Rented by the Quartermaster's Dept. at the Post of Santa Fe, New Mexico*, 32 Cong., 1st sess., *House Exec. Doc. 2*, 242.

5. Santa Fe County Probate Records, Bonds of Administrators and Guardians of Estate, Book A-1 1851–64, NMSA. Baptized in 1825 by his half-brother, José Eulogio Ortíz was the youngest son of Juan Rafael Ortíz and Gertrudis Pino. He became a priest, accompanied Lamy to Rome in 1854, and served in Taos 1856–57. Olmsted, "Ortiz Family of New Mexico," typescript, NMSA.

6. Chaves Letter, NMSA. Amado Chaves was the son of Manuel Antonio Chaves and Vicente Labadie.

7. Laughlin, *The Wind Leaves No Shadow*, 336.

8. Espinosa to Amigo Phil [St. George Cooke], Albuquerque, N.Mex., Mar. 25, [n.y.], and Espinosa to Jenkins, Albuquerque, N.Mex., May 10 and 11, 1968; Jenkins to Espinosa, Santa Fe, May 9, 1968, History File 80, NMSA.

9. Dehon was the maiden name of Wheaton's mother. Theodore Wheaton received a salary of $125 as a circuit attorney for the Third Judicial District for the six months, June 29 to Dec. 29, 1848. On Aug. 26, 1851, he was admitted to practice law in the U.S. district courts of the Territory of New Mexico by Chief Justice Grafton Baker. TANM, 46:14; U.S. District Court Records 1850–56, NMSA.

10. Theodore Dehon Wheaton was born Aug. 16, 1813, in Newport, R.I. In 1838, after teaching school in Saline County, Mo., Wheaton lived in St. Joseph where he practiced law and was one of three lawyers, along with David Atchison and Alexander Doniphan, admitted to the bar in Platte County, Mar. 25, 1839. Wheaton was a law partner of Senator and U.S. Vice President David R. Atchison. *History of Saline County, Missouri*, 440; *History of Buchanan County, Missouri*, 231; *History of Andrew and De Kalb Counties, Missouri*, 111. By 1844 Wheaton had moved from St. Joseph to Savannah, Mo., where he was practicing law. Wheaton to Sappington, Savannah, Mar. 6, 1844, UM-MSHS. From 1854 to 1858 Theodore Wheaton served as New Mexico's fifth attorney general; from 1861 to 1866 he was U.S. attorney general. At the opening of his tenure as attorney general he suffered a case of smallpox in 1861. Hunt, *Kirby Benedict, Frontier Federal Judge*, 156; Anderson, *History of New Mexico*, 266. Wheaton's first

wife was Catarina Vigil (?) by whom he had several children; his second wife, Margaret McCarthy, died in 1863. Interview with Bertha Wheaton Gatlin Mascareñas (granddaughter of T. D. Wheaton and daughter of Leandro Wheaton and Clotilde Romero) Apr. 8, 1988. Mention is made concerning the possible opening of a school in the house of Theodore Wheaton in Taos, where three of Carson's sons would attend. Simmons, *Kit Carson and His Three Wives*, 106. For a time, Wheaton was a member of the law firm of Houghton, Wheaton, and Smith in Santa Fe. He died of Brights Disease near Ocaté, N.Mex., Dec. 22, 1873. Unidentified and undated newspaper clipping, NHS; History File No. 106, NMSA.

11. *Barcelo v. Coalter* [Coulter], U.S. District Court Records, Sept. 17, 1850, NMSA. The United States Hotel soon became known as the Exchange Hotel and ultimately La Fonda Hotel. In 1848, $500 is recorded as the gambling license fee in the county of Santa Fe. TANM, 46:17.

12. Ritch Coll., roll 9, NMSA.

13. Ibid. Kearny's organic code was the law concerning registers of land. Gen. Stephen Watts Kearny failed to mention Wheaton's name and credited the code to Col. Alexander Doniphan, who claimed to have received assistance from private Willard P. Hall of his regiment. Kearny to Adjutant General, Sept. 22, 1846, NA. In 1847 an adjutant to Major Lewis Clark's Battalion Missouri Light Artillery, Lieut. Christian Kribben, wrote that "Gen. Kearny and Col. Doniphan framed and collated a certain kind of code of laws for the government of the territory which was partly taken from the statues of Missouri and from the Spanish and Mexican code now existing." Letters of Christian Cribben [Kribben], Mexican War Coll., MHS; Connelley, *Doniphan's Expedition*, 573. See Prince, *The General Laws of New Mexico*. Kribben was a correspondent of the *Die Täglicher Anzeiger des Westerns* and the *Daily Missouri Republican*.

14. Ritch Coll., roll 9, NMSA.

15. TANM, 21:29.

16. Information regarding Wheaton and the Navajos courtesy of Richard Salazar, former state archivist.

17. *History of Buchanan County*, 231.

18. Twitchell, *Old Santa Fe*, 338; Chaves Letter, NMSA. No record of excommunication has been found in church records. Twitchell describes Manuel Antonio as a musical, "intrepid old gentlemen, a singer of comic songs." Amado Chaves gives the name of José Cisneros y Lucero, rather than Manuel Antonio, his brother. José Miguel Cisneros, also the son of María Rita Lucero and Hermenegildo Cisneros, was three years older than Manuel Antonio. Sisneros, *Herencia*, 20.

19. Clark, *Community of Property and the Family in New Mexico*, 3, 6. Not until 1876 did the territorial legislature establish the common law as a matter of practice and decision.

20. The 1870 U.S. Census for Valencia County gives 1815 as María de la Luz's birth year, which she confirms in her marriage diligencia.

21. Sunder, *Matt Field on the Santa Fe Trail*, 206. The young girl seen riding with Tules may have been Rafaela (Pino) Barceló, who was born ca. 1828 and listed as a servant on the 1850 U.S. Census for Santa Fe. Rafaela gave birth to a son on Jan. 23, 1845, named José Manuel Pino, and to a daughter on Feb. 5, 1847, named María de la Luz Blasa, father unknown in both instances. Santa Fe Baptisms, AASF, 17:404, 524. Rafaela, described as "family of Da. Gertrudis Barceló," died on Apr. 29, 1851. Santa Fe Burials, AASF, 41:235.

22. Dr. Ward Alan Minge generously allowed me to photograph the comb, now in the Museum of Albuquerque Collection. The monte table from Taos, said to have once belonged to Tules, is owned by Laughlin Barker, son of author Ruth Laughlin. The petaca and chalice are in the Museum of Spanish Colonial Art in Santa Fe. In 1940 red-haired Rafaela Hinojosa de Maldonado, neighbor of the author, portrayed Doña Tules in the entrada of the Coronado Quartrocentennial Celebration. AJ, Feb. 2, 1994.

23. Santa Fe County District Court Records, Civil Cases 1852, Case 383, NMSA; U.S. District Court Records, First Judicial District, 1850–53. The literate Santiago Flores signs the court document.

24. First Judicial District Court, Santa Fe County 1850–53, 282, NMSA.

25. Santa Fe County Records, Probate Court Journal 1848–53, 153, NMSA. Josiah Gregg comments on the *tenazitas de oro* (little golden tongs) used by the Mexican women to hold their cigarettes to avoid nicotine stains on their fingers. In 1846 Susan Magoffin mentions the "necklaces, countless rings, combs." Magoffin, *Down the Santa Fe Trail*, 124. See Egan, *Relicarios*.

26. The Santa Fe County Records, Probate Court Journal, 1848–56, recorded the bail for Pedro Mondragón as $1,000; in the indictment of the First Judicial Court the bail was listed as $500.

27. This may have been James Barry, formerly a clerk at Bent's Fort in 1838, and perhaps one of four men who traveled to Santa Fe with Matt Field in 1839. Barry, *Beginning of the West*, 352, 374.

28. U.S. Census 1870 for Valencia County. On this same census Rumaldo Sánches, son of María de la Luz and age thirty-eight, indicated that he could both read and write.

29. Tomé Marriages, AASF, 33:917.

30. Surveyor General Report No. 21, Town of Tajique Grant, NMSA; District Court Records, Torrance County, Civil Case No. 110, NMSA.

31. Tomé Marriages, AASF, 33:917; Chávez, *New Mexico Roots*, Diligencia Matrimonial no. 52, 9:1716.

32. Manuel Rafael Sanches, father of Juan Rafael, was one of the original Tajique land grantees. Tajique, a small village in Torrance County south

of Chililí at the eastern foot of the Manzano Mountains, is thought to have been abandoned in the late seventeenth century because of Apache raids.

33. Tomé Baptisms, AASF, 24:320, 367, 428, 489, 598, and 879; Tomé Burials, AASF, 43:1128. Tomé Baptisms, 24:561. Dolores Barceló was the mother of Tules. The 1900 U.S. Census for Valencia County records Pablo Sanches y Barceló, born May 1840, living in Tajique; and also a Jesús Sanches y Barceló, born Jan. 1844.

34. The 1850 and 1860 U.S. censuses of New Mexico, Valencia County. Of interest is that the newly ordained Padre Antonio José Martínez from Taos baptized the Sanches children in place of the absent Padre Madariaga.

35. An adult son José of Manuel Sanches was buried on Oct. 28, 1848, possibly Juan Rafael. A son Juan Rafael II was born Nov. 21, 1847. Tomé Burials, AASF, 43:1307; Administración del estado de la difunto María de la Luz Barcelo, Valencia County Probate Journal A, 214–17, NMSA.

36. Santa Fe Baptisms, AASF, 16:1261. Rallitos was one month old when baptized.

37. Ibid. AASF, 31:868. María Petra Gutierres was born July 18, 1823, to Gabriel Gutierres and Dolores Cisneros, a sister-in-law of Tules. Sandia Baptisms, AASF, 8:615. Petra died at Puerto de Luna, N.Mex., Dec. 27, 1890. Petra and Rallitos (mother and daughter) were raised by Tules. Petra Giddings Riddle Interview 1994. Provided Rallitos was a full-term pregnancy, the conception of Rallitos would have occurred in Apr. 1837. For a study on the name "Rayos" given to girl babies born in New Mexico between 1833 and 1837, see David Snow, "Nuestra Señora del Rayo," typescript, CC. Relevant to the birth of Rallitos, a caravan of 80 wagons and 160 men carrying $150,000 of merchandise arrived in Santa Fe from Missouri in May 1837. Barry, *Beginning of the West*, 325.

38. Chávez Letter, NMSA. Tules no doubt attended one or more of the nine major fairs in Mexico: Aguas Calientes, Allende in Chihuahua, Chilapa, Chilpanzingo, Huejutla, Cuidad Guerrero, Saltillo, San Juan de los Lagos, and Tenancingo. Early New Mexico fairs lasting eight or twelve days at Las Vegas, Mesilla, Tomé, Las Cruces, Albuquerque, Socorro, and Santa Fe were legally established by the legislature of 1852–55; these acts, however, were repealed in 1856–57. Bancroft, *History of Arizona and New Mexico*, 17:644.

39. Petra Giddings Riddle Interview, 1994.

40. Gertrudis Barceló was a godparent at the baptism of Lorenzo Labadie in 1825. Tomé Baptisms, AASF, 24:357. Lorenzo was the descendant of Frenchman Domingo Labadie.

41. Petra Giddings Riddle Interview, 1994.

42. John MacRae Washington was born to Baily and Euphan (Wallace)

Washington at his father's estate, Windsor Forest, in Stafford County, Va., in Oct. 1797. His father was a second cousin of George Washington. A graduate of the U.S. Military Academy in 1817, he married Fanny MacRae early in his career, who was a daughter of Dr. Jack MacRae, nephew of Col. William Washington, the brother of Baily Washington. From 1833 to 1838 John MacRae Washington engaged in the Creek and Florida wars against the Seminoles at Locha-Hatchee; he later participated in the battle of Buena Vista, Feb. 22, 1847, during the U.S.–Mexican War. DAB, 19:528–29; Simpson, *Navaho Expedition*, xliv–xlv.

43. The room in the Palace of the Governors was that of the New Mexico Historical Society. Petra Giddings Riddle Interview, 1994. A William Washington Garrard, who was born in June 1762 died in Dec. 1835, suggests the name recalled by Petra Giddings Riddle but the incorrect chronology of the mystery. See Simpson, *Navaho Expedition*, xliv.

44. NYDTi, Jan. 14, 1854. Also on board the San Francisco were Companies A, B, D, G, H, I, K, and L of the Third Regiment of the U.S. Artillery. Under Jefferson Davis, secretary of war, a board of inquiry was convened composed of Maj. Gen. Winfield Scott, commanding the army; Bvt. Brig. Gen. Henry Stanton, asst. quartermaster general; Bvt. Col. E. V. Sumner, Lieut. Col. First Dragoons; and Bvt. Maj. John F. Lee, judge advocate of the army, as recorder.

45. Ritch Coll., roll 1, NMSA. It is unclear which name is the surname.

46. In ruling out other possible men with the name of Garrard, Lewis H. Garrard, author of *Wah-to-yah and the Taos Trail* (1850), seventeen at the time of his trip to New Mexico in 1846, would have been only eight or nine years old when Rallitos was conceived in 1837.

47. In Jan. 2006 I interviewed Margaret Racel, age 100, the great-granddaughter of Rallitos Labadie. Unable to recall certain events clearly, of course, Racel's physical coloring—fair skin and blue eyes—is intriguing. There may be truth to the long-standing belief that Col. John Washington indeed fathered Rallitos Sisneros de Labadie.

48. It is interesting to note that in July 1831 William Baxter Giddings ("y Elliott"), son of James M. Giddings, received guía no. 56. Ritch Coll., roll 1, NMSA.

49. Col. John M. Washington, born Oct. 17, 1797, newly appointed military commander and provisional governor for N.Mex., left Monterrey, Mex., July 26 or 28, 1848, and arrived in Santa Fe on Oct. 10, 1848. Barry, *Beginning of the West*, 785; Espinosa, "Memoir of a Kentuckian in New Mexico," NMHR 13:4. Between 1836 and 1838, then captain John Washington fought in the Creek and Florida wars against the Seminole Indians. DAB, 19:528–29.

50. Santa Fe Baptisms, AASF, 16:994. The word *legitimate* following the name of Rallitos in the marriage entry is crossed out by Father José de Jesús

Luján, pastor of the Parroquia. Lorenzo Labadie, according to his cast metal tombstone found by the author in the Campo Santo del Calvario at Puerto de Luna, was born Aug. 10, 1823. The son of Pablo Labadie and Rosa Sisneros of Valencia, Lorenzo died on his eighty-first birthday, Aug. 10, 1904. AJ, Aug. 12, 1904.

51. Santa Fe Marriages, AASF, 31:122–23.

52. DNM, Feb. 3, 1893; SFNM, Aug. 14, 1900. No gravestone has been found for Rallitos.

53. Santa Fe Baptisms, AASF, 17:577. Lucius Falkland Thruston, a Kentuckian, was born in Louisville, Kentucky, on July 18, 1799, to John Thruston and Elizabeth Thruston Whiting, who were cousins. Susan Magoffin wrote that Thruston "has spent many years in this country in different parts; . . . I suspect he has become so well iniciated [*sic*] in the *manners of living and ways* of Mexico, he will not be in much of a hurry to visit his native land." Magoffin, *Down the Santa Fe Trail*, 106 m. 38, 126–27; SLR, Mar. 1, 1847; TANM 46:18. Lucius Thruston was one of several Santa Fe merchants eager to open a shorter and seasonably more favorable route through Texas, thus rerouting the Chihuahua and Santa Fe trade. Bieber, *Southern Trails to California in 1849*, 5:141–42.

54. Santa Fe County Records, Deed Book D, 537.

55. Jemez Baptisms, AASF, 5:847. In 1791, twenty-year-old Francisco Griego is listed as a farmer in Santa Fe, originally from Río Abajo. Census of 1790, SANM II, 12:398. The marriage record of Trinidad and Dolores Griego is yet to be found.

56. "Old Santa Fe," 1:273 n262. See also Trinidad Barceló letters concerning regulations and other mining matters in 1846. SANM I, 6:67, 1108.

57. Taos Baptisms, AASF, 20:118; Taos Burials, AASF, 42:181. Dolores Griego also buried a child named José Carmen in October 1851, no father given. Santa Fe Burials, AASF, 41:211.

58. *U.S. v. Trinidad Barceló et al.*, History File 11, NMSA; Treason Trial of Trinidad Barceló, Mar. 1847, History File 166, NMSA. District Court Records of the treason trials may be found in the Santa Fe County treasurer's Warrant Book 1848–54, NMSA.

59. See chapter 1, n3.

60. Bernalillo County Records, Probate Book A, 320; Bernalillo County Records, Direct Index, reel 1 (1848–89), BCC, Albuquerque. Dolores Griego was perhaps buried in the Mountain Road Cemetery. Around 1871–72 two tons of bones were moved from this cemetery to the Santa Barbara Cemetery. Courtesy of David Snow, Museum of New Mexico. Although W. G. Ritch stated that Dolores Griego died in the Armijo House in Albuquerque (there were four or more), real estate records indicate that she owned a house and land on the old town plaza. Bernalillo County Records, Deed Book H, 80, NMSA. Dolores Griego also owned

a seven-room house a block north of the Santa Fe residence of Tules, which was sold to Oliver P. Hovey. In the deed, marked and signed with her "x," Griego is described as a resident of Bernalillo County in Mar. 1858. Santa Fe County Records, Deed Book B, 335–36. In 1858 "Doleres Griezo de Barcelo" claimed that 115 goats and sheep, and two oxen, valued at $270, were stolen by Navajo Indians in 1847. U.S. Sen. Doc., Ex. Doc. No. 55, 35th Congress, 1st Sess., Report of the Secretary of Interior upon Claims for Depredations by Indians in the Territory of New Mexico, May 12, 1858; Santa Fe Census for 1841, 30:350, MANM; "Old Santa Fe," 1:27; *International Genealogical Index*, LDS, Baptismal Records of Nuestra Señora del Rosario Parish, Moctezuma, Sonora, Mexico.

61. Ritch Coll., roll 1, NMSA. This suggests that Dolores Griego traveled with the soldiers.

62. Judicial Proceedings, Jusgado 1° of Santa Fe, Book of Conciliations, MANM, 26:617.

63. U.S. 1850 Census for Santa Fe.

64. Judge Santiago Campos Notes, CC.

65. Santa Fe Baptisms, AASF, 17:205. Giddings is recorded as "Santiago Carlos."

66. James Madison Giddings was born Mar. 26, 1806, to George Giddings and Frances Tandy. U.S. District Court Judge Santiago Campos, great-grandson of James M. Giddings, generously assisted me in obtaining the biographical and genealogical history, as well as photos of Rallitos, Petra, and James M. Giddings. With the assistance of a court reporter, Judge Campos and I interviewed ninety-year-old Petra Giddings Riddle, daughter of William Baxter Giddings, who was born June 8, 1894, and present at the death in 1900 of Rayitos Gutierres Labadie. Oliva, *Fort Union and the Frontier Army in the Southwest*, 58–59.

67. Jaramillo, *Shadows of the Past*, 91–92. Cleofas was a niece of Gaspar Ortíz y Alarid.

68. The identity of Francisca remains unknown.

69. Santa Fe Marriages, AASF, 31:1107. Her name is recorded as Carmen, "familiar de D. Manuel Sisneros & Da Gertrudis Barcelo," and signed by P. Machebeuf, seminary friend of Bishop Jean Baptiste Lamy. Peter Derr wrote "Account of Experience with First Overland Train on Southern Route from Salt Lake," called the Gruwell-Derr Train (1849). Derr Ms., BL. The Derr family settled in Humbolt County, Calif.

70. Petermann to Cook, June 26, 1991.

71. De Marle had returned to Germany in 1848.

72. U.S. Census for New Mexico 1860; declaration of citizenship, U.S. District Court Records, First Judicial District, 1851–52, NMSA; SFWG, June 11, 1853, Dec. 25, 1858; Towne, "Printing in New Mexico," NMHR, 35:116; SFWG, Nov. 2, 1867; Santa Fe Burials, AASF, 88:66. Jewish merchant

William Zeckendorf of Albuquerque, N.Mex., noted that "delegate
Chávez" struck "a helpless crippled man, Augustin De Marle, one of
the most intelligent citizens Santa Fe ever had, with a cane because he
defended the Jews." SFWG, June 22, 1867.

73. Sunder, *Matt Field on the Santa Fe Trail*, 208.
74. Jaramillo, *Shadows of the Past*, 93.
75. Cabeza de Baca, "Don Gaspar Ortiz y Alari—Alcalde and Piñon King,"
The Santa Fe Scene, Sept. 13, 1958, 24–25; Read, *Illustrated History of New
Mexico*, 771; Ellis, "Fraud without Scandal: The Roque Lovato Grand and
Gaspar Ortiz y Alarid," NMHR, 57:43–62; SFDNM, July 11, 1882.
76. Olmsted, "The Ortiz Family of New Mexico," 40, NMSA.
77. Read, *Illustrated History of New Mexico*, 538.
78. Olmsted, "The Ortiz Family of New Mexico," NMSA; "Old Santa Fe,"
2:141. An alcalde was a civil official with judicial, executive, and legislative
functions. See Simmons, *Spanish Government in New Mexico*, 219.
79. Dr. Charles McDougall was born in Chillicothe, Ohio, Sept. 21, 1804.
In 1850 McDougall had relieved Dr. Lewis A. Edwards at Fort Marcy.
Following his retirement in 1869 with the rank of Brig. Gen., U.S. Army,
he died at Fairfield, Clark County, Va., July 25, 1885. Heitman, *Historical
Register and Dictionary of the U.S. Army, 1789–1903*, 663. Dr. McDougall
is buried beside his wife, Maria Hanson, who died Aug. 19, 1876. Both are
buried in the OBG (old burial ground) of Jefferson Barracks, St. Louis,
Mo. The author visited Fairfield, McDougall's eighteenth-century estate
outside of Berryville, Va., near Washington, D.C. The large stone colonial
mansion is on the National Register of Historic Places due to its association with President George Washington, who on several occasions visited
his first cousin Warner Washington, then owner of Fairfield. National
Register of Historic Places Inventory-Nomination Form, State of Virginia,
U.S. Dept. of the Interior, NPS.
80. Emmett, *Fort Union and the Winning of the Southwest*, 146–47.
81. McCall, *New Mexico in 1850: A Military View*, 119.
82. Chaput, *François X. Aubry*, 112–13.
83. Morris Diary, UVL Ms. 3448:22.
84. McParlin to Mother & Brother, Albuquerque, N.Mex., Jan. 24, 1851,
McParlin Letters, GHC.
85. Kephart to Whipple, Feb. 20, 1851, ARC.
86. Withers, "Letters of a College Boy," MHS Bulletin 6:12.
87. Bowen, "My Dear Mother," Sept. 2, 1851, AC.
88. "Old Santa Fe," 1:246n186, 264.
89. Townley, "El Placer: A New Mexico Mining Boom Before 1846," JOW
10:108; Juan B. Vigil List of Santa Fe Property Owners 1836. SANM I, roll
6, 1227–29.

90. Espinosa, "Memoir of a Kentuckian in New Mexico 1848–1884," NMHR 13:1–13.
91. Parrish, "The German Jew," NMHR 35:3.
92. Manuel Valdes Account, Read Collection 306a, NMSA.
93. Chávez, *Manuel Alvarez*, 9, 13, 17, 31, 20, 190. Joseph Mercure testified that Alvarez had sired three sons (one of whom died) by an Indian wife. According to Mercure, on his return from Europe in Dec. 1855, Alvarez had seen his sons in Spain. Ocaté Land Claim, Land Grant Records, 26:777, NMSA.
94. Santa Fe Burials, AASF, 88:34. Etienne Avel arrived in New Mexico in 1854 from the Auvergne region in central France.
95. SFWG, Dec. 26, 1857.
96. Weigle, *Brothers of Light, Brothers of Blood*, 24–25. Bishop of Durango, José Antonio Laureano de Zubiría, first visited New Mexico in 1833, making his second visit in 1845 and his last in 1850. Padre Martínez described the lay brotherhood of penitents in 1833, which he called "Penitentes." In his letter dated July 21, 1833, from Santa Cruz de la Cañada (north of Santa Fe), Zubiría expressed his opposition to Penitente groups. See also Gregg, *Commerce of the Prairies*, 181n7; and Wroth, *Images of Penance, Images of Mercy*, Appendix I, 172. Twenty-four paupers lowered the corpse of the wealthy Spanish merchant Pero Hernández de Portillo into the earth. See Bartolomé Bennassar, *The Spanish Character: Attitudes and Mentalities from the Sixteenth to the Nineteenth Century* (Berkeley: University of California Press, 1979).
97. Despite Thomas Chávez's hypothesis in his biography, the place of Alvarez's burial remains in question. Chávez, *Manuel Alvarez*, 190. In May 2004 the author traveled to Monterrey, Mex., in search of the tombstone of Alvarez. Joseph Mercure, a witness on July 6, 1856, died near the Arkansas River in Nov. 1863. His remains were returned to Santa Fe to be buried at the San Miguel Mission. Mercure had acquired considerable wealth and had known Alvarez since 1848. SFWG, Aug. 15, Sept. 5, Sept. 19, and Nov. 14, 1863; Ocaté Land Claim, Land Grant Records, reel 26:777.
98. See Cook, "¿Porque Monterrey?" *Wagon Tracks* 19:6–9.
99. Jenkins, "The Donaciano Vigil House," *Bulletin of the Historic Santa Fe Foundation* 12:1–9.

Notes to Chapter 7

1. The title of this chapter recalls the Latin words inscribed on a stone sundial constructed in Santa Fe's plaza by Governor don Antonio Narbona (1825–27). It was the only public clock at the time; Barreiro, *Ojeada*, 13. Another sundial was constructed in the plaza in 1847 by Lt. Alexander B. Dyer (1815–74), who fought in the uprising at Embudo and Taos. Journal of A. B. Dyer, ACHLA. Author Ruth Laughlin wrote in her novel: "The

puny cries of men in his land are like the wind that travels swiftly before the sun but leaves no shadow." Laughlin, *The Wind Leaves No Shadow*, 200.

2. See Aurora Lucero-White, "El Velorio," WPA File 5-5-21 no. 21, ACHLA. As noted, Bishop Jean Baptiste Lamy returned to Santa Fe from Durango on Jan. 10, 1852, six or seven days prior to the death of Doña Tules. However, vicar general Machebeuf had expected his return by Christmas. Loose Documents, AASF, 5:171.

3. Chávez Letter, NMSA. Guadalupe Tafoya was the mother-in-law of Carlos [Charles] Conklin (son of Juana Ortiz and James Conklin), and the second wife of Tomás Valencia, a well-known trader, gambler, and hatmaker from Sonora. Chávez, "A Kind and Gentle Life," CC; Taos Marriages, AASF, 32:907; Santa Fe Marriages, AASF, 89: n.f.; McGaw, *Savage Scene*, 102.

4. *Alabados*: songs.

5. "Arroyo Hondo," *El Palacio*, 81:16.

6. Letter from Santa Fe, MDR, Dec. 2, 1852.

7. "From Santa Fe" in MDR, from the *Daily Alta*, Calif., Jan. 19, 1852.

8. The decorative crenellation of the Parroquia parapets was yet to occur and may have been the influence of the French Vicar General J. B. Machebeuf. Ellis, *Bishop Lamy's Cathedral*, 188n18.

9. SFNM, Feb. 20, 1877.

10. Author Ruth Laughlin reminisced that one of her earliest memories was her mother's story of Lamy's bier being carried around the plaza "as a farewell blessing to his people." SFNM, Aug. 3, 1958.

11. Jaramillo, *Shadows of the Past*, 92.

12. Santa Fe Burials, AASF, 41:275.

13. Dickinson to E. Kern, Jan. 27, 1851 [1852], ACHL. Dickinson also wrote that a local Indian agent had come down with the "inflamatory [*sic*] *two step*" caused, he claimed, "by the exposure to the cold, bugs, lice, & squaws, very dangerous antagonists sometimes." A native of the state of New York, Horace L. Dickinson arrived in Santa Fe in 1848; he served as probate judge of Santa Fe County, fourth clerk of the Legislative Council, private secretary to the governor, and auditor of public accounts for the Territory of New Mexico. He died of typhoid at age thirty-one. SFWG, Jan. 5, 1856.

14. Davis, *El Gringo*, 185–86, 220.

15. Talbot Journal, June 25 and July 8, 1863, EAD. Fray Angélico Chávez viewed these accounts as "fancifully reputed." Chávez, "Doña Tules," *El Palacio*, 57:227–34.

16. Davis, *El Gringo*, 185–86; Talbot Journal, July 8, 1863, EAD. Eleven years later Bishop Talbot wrote the following: the "bishops bill on record in court as paid by this [*sic*] executors, made out in regular form by himself

and amounting to $1597.00." The funeral expense of a "young Mexican" four years later in 1856, the bill of which is described as made out in "mercantile form," was in the amount of $141.00, though without an in-church burial. Fábricas ranged from *de limosna*, or free of charge, to thirty-eight pesos, the more common being one or two pesos.

17. Ralph Emerson Twitchell in *Old Santa Fe*, 339n611, cited W. W. Davis in *El Gringo*, 186, giving the amount of $1,000 paid to the bishop and $50 for each paso or stop, which might have totaled $150 had there been three pasos.

18. MDR, Mar. 4, 1852. NYDT, Mar. 17, 1852. Horgan wrote, "Although done in Lamy's name, the obsequies, according to later evidence, seemed to have been the work of [Juan Felipe] Ortiz, the rural dean." Horgan, *Lamy*, 186. A remote relationship existed between Tules and the vicar by the marriage of her mother to an unnamed son or nephew of the noted Don Pedro Bautista Pino through Gertrudis Pino, who in 1816 became the second stepmother of Juan Felipe Ortíz. Chávez, *Origins of New Mexico Families*, 259–60, 328, 330. Fray Angélico Chávez described the funeral "from church records the actual . . . details of her obsequies and burial costs." Chávez, "Dona Tules," *El Palacio*, 57:227–35. The records Fray Angélico referred to have not been found. Because no fábrica, burial costs, or funeral details were recorded, one is apt to wonder if Chávez indeed saw the controversial "bishop's bill." Four south chapel burials occurred in 1847. Ellis, *Bishop Lamy's Cathedral*, 75–77, 184.

19. Santa Fe Burials, AASF, 41:65; Alvarez Papers, folder 18, NMSA. On the reverse of a draft ad for registration by Guillermo C. Skinner is a funeral notice for Rosa Genobeva Flores dated June 14, 1847. Don Antonio José Ortíz donated the Chapel of San Antonio de Padua. In 1797 Ortíz requested that he and members of his family be buried in the south chapel, constructed at his own expense. Ellis, *Bishop Lamy's Cathedral*, 61. By 1876 burials within any church were forbidden by law. SFNM, Feb. 8, 1876.

20. Santa Fe Baptisms, AASF, 17:505. A James Cole, along with Santiago Flores and James Giddings, contributed five pesos to a patriotic celebration in 1844. MANM, 37:564. An ornate altar was donated by Nellie Riordan Mulligan as a memorial for her husband, who died in 1917. SFNM, Sept. 27, 1957. In 1940 my first pipe organ lessons, under Elsie Hammond, were in St. Francis Cathedral. I recall St. Anthony chapel's "wedding cake" altar and the dank odor of the mud floor.

21. Abert, *Report of Lieut. J. W. Abert*, 417–548.

22. Allison, "Santa Fe in 1846," *Old Santa Fe* 2:401–2.

23. Loose Documents 1850–51, AASF; Chávez and Chávez, *Wake for a Fat Vicar*, 93, 96. See also Hinchey diary. Prior to his departure to Durango in Sept. 1851, Lamy had employed E. Noël as a schoolmaster. It is not known

if this was the same Noël, according to Horgan, involved in a Mora scandal, who disappeared after the mysterious poisoning of Father Etienne Avel. Horgan, *Lamy*, 260. See also Hanks, *Lamy's Legion: The Individual Histories of Secular Clergy Serving in the Archdiocese of Santa Fe from 1850 to 1912.*

24. Lane, *I Married a Soldier*, 115; Magoffin, *Down the Santa Fe Trail*, 137.

25. Ellis, *Bishop Lamy's Cathedral*, 67.

26. Ibid., 60–61; Sena, "The Chapel of Don Antonio José Ortiz," NMHR 13:347–59.

27. Architectural historians George Kubler and S. G. Morley hypothesized that the original south chapel of La Parroquia at some point was completely torn down and rebuilt. Kubler, *Religious Architecture of New Mexico*, 9; Kingsbury to Webb, Santa Fe, July 26, 1853, J. Webb Papers, MHS.

28. Ellis, *Bishop Lamy's Cathedral*, 108–9.

29. The location of this painting mentioned by Ruth Laughlin remains unknown today. Barker, *Caballeros*, 183.

30. A number of old Santa Feans recount that Tules's remains were moved to an old camposanto "outside the north wall" of the Parroquia or else to a cemetery immediately south of today's Masonic Lodge (Montezuma No. 1). The latter area is unlikely because it was a Protestant cemetery. Early Santa Fean Ramona Latimer recalled the exhumation of a grave near today's City Hall at Marcy and Lincoln Streets. She told of seeing a coffin holding an elaborately dressed woman whom she believed was Doña Tules. It remains unlikely that her remains were moved from La Parroquia. The author interviewed surviving workmen who say they found no remains of an adult woman.

31. Ellis, *Bishop Lamy's Cathedral*, 34, 36.

32. MDR, Mar. 27, 1852.

33. Chávez, "Doña Tules," *El Palacio*, 57:233.

34. See Cook, *Loretto: The Sisters and Their Santa Fe Chapel* (2002). In 1851 Lamy traveled from Cincinnati to New Orleans to San Antonio to El Paso and northward up El Camino Real del Tierra Adentro, rather than crossing the Santa Fe Trail.

35. Both Machebeuf and the young Projectus Mouly, architect of Loretto Chapel, were named after St. Priest, the patron saint of Volvic, France. Both proceeded to use the Latin equivalent of their names to avoid confusion.

36. Santa Fe Marriages, AASF, 31:1116.

37. Santa Fe County Deed Book C, 105.

38. Courtesy of Anna Belle Cartwright, Kansas City, Mo. An item in the SFWG, July 29, 1854, relates that two towers on the Catholic Church on the plaza (probably La Castrense) were being built. William James Hinchey was born Dec. 5, 1829, in Dublin, Ireland. In 1856 he opened

a studio in St. Louis, where he was befriended by painters Manuel de Franco and George Caleb Bingham, and became a successful portraitist. He died in September 1893 after being thrown from a cable car.

39. The remaining walls of La Castrense, photographed by Irene Smelser Straw (author's mother), were demolished in the mid-1950s.

40. Burr, *The Golden Quicksand*; Grant, *Doña Lona*; Laughlin, *The Wind Leaves No Shadow*; Sabin, *The Rose of Santa Fe*; Seton, *The Turquoise*; musical: score and lyrics by Stewart *¡Viva Santa Fe!*; play, Sánchez, *Destiny's Darling*, n.d., CC; *Lubbock Avalanche-Journal*, Oct. 13, 1991.

Notes to Appendix A

1. Link Papers, MHS.

2. Maj. Meriwether Lewis Clark was the eldest son of William Clark of the famed Lewis and Clark expedition.

3. A discussion of the difficulty between the Santa Fe and Chihuahua Trails traders and Lt. Colonel D. D. Mitchell is found in Glasgow and Glasgow, *Brothers on the Santa Fe and Chihuahua Trails*, 120, 120n116.

4. Capt. Philip St. George Cooke was born in Va. in 1809, graduating from West Point in 1827. He died in 1873. Connelley, *Doniphan's Expedition*, 264n60.

5. For a discussion of the conflict between Kearny and Fremont see Harlow, *California Conquered: War and Peace on the Pacific*. Gen. S. W. Kearny arrested Col. Fremont on charges of mutiny, disobedience of the lawful command of a superior officer, and conduct to the prejudice of good order and military discipline. Fremont rejected a presidential offer of clemency in the belief that it would be an admission of guilt. He then resigned from the army.

6. This may have been Benjamin Walker named in the Maxwell Land Grant suit later brought by his Mo. heirs. Brayer, *William Blackmore*, 1:129n11. The widow of the wealthy trader Antonio José Chávez, murdered in 1843, was Barbara Armijo, a niece of Mexican governor Manuel Armijo. Simmons, *Murder on the Santa Fe Trail*, 3.

7. The rumor proved false.

8. Jules De Mun Papers, MHS.

9. Six children survived Martha and Lt. Col. D. D. Mitchell: Fanny, Mary, Susan, David D., Jr., Taylor S., and Charles G.

10. Born in the District of Columbia, Maj. Richard Hanson Weightman graduated from West Point. Following the Mexican War he came to Santa Fe where he operated a newspaper and practiced law. Weightman stabbed François X. Aubry in the Mercure store on the south side of the Santa Fe plaza during an argument. Connelley, *Doniphan's Expedition*, 361n83.

Note to Appendix C

1. See Santa Fe County District Court, Civil Cases No. 241 and No. 383, NMSA. A fictional account of this encounter in the U.S. Hotel may be found in Laughlin, *The Wind Leaves No Shadow*, 343–44.

Bibliography

Abbreviations

AASF	Archives of the Archdiocese of Santa Fe
AC	Arrott Collection
ACHLA	Angélico Chávez History Library and Archives
AJ	*Albuquerque Journal*
APD	Archives of Puy-de-Dôme
ARC	Amistad Research Center
BCC	Bernalillo County Courthouse
BdeL	Bibliothéque de Lempdes
BL	Bancroft Library, University of California
CC	Cook Collection
CD	Consular Dispatches
DA	Durango Archives
DAB	*Dictionary of American Biography*
DNM	*Daily New Mexican*
EAD	Episcopal Archdiocese Archives
GHC	Gary Hendershott Collection
JOW	*Journal of the West*
LDS	Church of the Latter-day Saints
MANM	Mexican Archives of New Mexico

MDR	*Missouri Daily Republican*
MHS	Missouri Historical Society
NA	National Archives
NHS	Newport Historical Society
NMHR	*New Mexico Historical Review*
NMSA	New Mexico State Archives & Library
NPS	National Park Service
NYDT	*New York Daily Tribune*
NYDTi	*New York Daily Times*
NYHS	New York Historical Society
SANM	Spanish Archives of New Mexico
SFNM	*Santa Fe New Mexican*
SFR	*Santa Fe Reporter*
SFWG	*Santa Fe Weekly Gazette*
SHQ	*Southwestern Historical Quarterly*
SLML	St. Louis Mercantile Library
SLR	*St. Louis Reveille*
TANM	Territorial Archives of New Mexico
UA	University of Arizona
UM-MSHS	University of Missouri–Missouri State Historical Society
UNC	University of North Carolina
UVL	University of Virginia Library
WHQ	*Western History Quarterly*

Archives

Amistad Research Center, Tulane University, New Orleans.
    William G. Kephart to George Whipple, Santa Fe, N.Mex., Feb. 20, 1851.
Archdiocese of Santa Fe, Archives.
    Baptisms, Burials, and Marriages. Jemez, Mora, Pojoaque, San Juan, Sandia, Santa Fe, Taos, and Tomé.
    Diligencias Matrimonias 1827, No. 54.
    Loose Documents, 1827, 1850–51.
Arrott Collection, Thomas C. Donnelly Library, Highlands University, Las Vegas, N.Mex.
    Catherine and Isaac Bowen Letters, 1851–53.
Bancroft Library, University of California, Berkeley.
    Peter Derr manuscript, "Account of Experience with First Overland Train on Southern Route from Salt Lake, 1849."
Bent's Fort, Fort Bent, Colorado.
    Untitled typescript.

Bernalillo County Records, Albuquerque.
  Deed Book H.
  Direct Index 1848–89.
  Probate Book A.
Angélico Chávez History Library and Archives, Museum of New Mexico.
  Journal of Lieutenant Alexander Brydie Dyer, 1846–47.
  Horace L. Dickinson to Edward Kern, Jan. 27, 1851[2], Ina Sizer Cassidy
    Collection.
  Aurora Lucero-White, "El Velorio," W.P.A. File 5-5-5, no. 1.
  Harry R. Rubenstein, "Chuza: A New Mexico Gambling Wheel," type-
    script, 1982.
Chávez, Fray Angélico.
  New Mexico Roots. Typescript index to the diligencias in the Archives of
    the Archdiocese of Santa Fe. Zimmerman Library, University of New
    Mexico, Albuquerque.
Church of the Latter-day Saints.
  Baptisms for Nuestra Señora del Rosario Parish, Moctezuma, Sonora,
    Oct. 8, 1860.
  International Genealogical Index, Parish of El Sagrario, Chihuahua,
    Mexico.
Colfax County Records, Raton, N.Mex.
  Civil Court Case 768, *Henry Clark v. The Maxwell Land Grant* 1886.
  Deed Book B.
  District Court, First Judicial District, Bill of Complaint.
Cook Collection.
  "Archival Report for Palace Ave.–Grant Ave.–Burro Alley Intersection,
    Santa Fe, New Mexico," Prepared by Nancy Hanks, Ph.D. Typescript,
    Apr. 3, 1995.
  U.S. District Court Judge Santiago E. Campos. Notes, n.d.
  Fray Angélico Chávez, Foreword to "A Kind and Gentle Life." Typescript,
    n.d.
  "Datos Biográficos de don Venancio Durazo Moreno." Typescript, n.d.
  August De Marle, "Rom." Typescript, 1845.
  Homer E. Milford, "Real de Dolores," Nomination for the Mining History
    Association's Year of Mining and Historic Preservation. Typescript,
    1999.
  Jane C. Sánchez, "Destiny's Darling." Typescript, 1992.
  David Snow, "Nuestra Señora del Rayo." Typescript, 2006.
Durango Archives, Mexico.
  Archivos del Ayuntamiento de Chihuahua, ca. 1712–13.
Episcopal Archdiocese Archives, Austin, Tex.
  Rt. Rev. Josiah Cruickshank Talbot Journals, 1856–82.

Gary Hendershott Collection, Little Rock, Ark.
  McParlin Letters. Dr. Thomas A. McParlin to mother & brother,
    Albuquerque, N.Mex., Jan. 24, 1851.
Lempdes, Bibliothéque de. France.
  Famille de Mgr. Jean-Baptiste Lamy.
Missouri Historical Society.
  Cribben [Kribben], Christian, Letters of, Mexican War Collection.
  De Mun, Jules, Papers.
  Ferguson, Philip Gooch, Diary.
  Link, Theodore, Papers.
  Mitchell, D. D., File Cards.
  Owens, Samuel C. Receipt, Santa Fe Papers, 1830–58.
  Santa Fe Papers, 1830–58.
  Webb, J., Papers, J. M. Kingsbury to Josiah J. Webb, Santa Fe, N.Mex., July
    26, 1853.
National Archives.
  Record Group 94, General Stephen Watts Kearny to Adjutant General,
    Sept. 22, 1846, Headquarters, Army of the West, Santa Fe, N.Mex.
  Record Group 199, Consular Dispatches, Vol. 1. Manuel Alvarez to James
    Buchanan, Sept. 4, 1846.
  Record Group 217, Accounts of Major Thomas Swords, Quartermaster.
  State Department, Territorial Papers, New Mexico 1851–72, W. W. H.
    Davis to Secretary of State, Sept. 25, 1857.
  National Register of Historic Places Inventory-Nomination Form, State of
    Virginia, U.S. Dept. of the Interior.
New Mexico State Archives & Library.
  Manuel Alvarez Papers.
Business Papers, 1852.
Folder 18, funeral notice for Rosa Bersabe Flores, June 14, 1847.
  Ledger, 1841–42.
  Chaves-Summers Papers, Amado Chaves Letter, Miscellaneous Historical
    Papers.
  Colfax County Records, Civil Court Case 768, *Henry Clark v. The
    Maxwell Land Grant* 1886.
  Doña Ana District, Civil Court Case 1854. Trinidad Barceló to D. Victor
    Baca, Huasabas, (Mexico), Oct. 31, 1853, in *Manuel Olona v. Victor
    Baca.*
  Dr. J. N. Dunlap, Diary 1847 [1846], Miscellaneous Letters and Diaries.
  Gilberto Espinosa, "Doña Tules: The Sharpest Monte Dealer in the
    Territory," in *Century,* n.d., Vertical File.
  Matt Field. Typescript of "Señora Toulous," Apr. 18, 1840, from *Daily New
    Orleans Picayune.*
  History Files 11, 80, 106, 166.

Mexican Archives of N.Mex.
    Census of Santa Fe, 1841.
Ocaté Land Grant Records.
Virginia L. Olmsted, "The Ortiz Family of New Mexico," typescript.
Benjamin Read Collection.
    Account of Bell Casting by Manuel Valdes, No. 306a.
    Reverse of No. 256.
William G. Ritch Collection.
Santa Fe County District Court Records.
    Civil Case no. 50 (1848).
    Civil Case no. 241 (1848).
    Civil Case no. 383 (1852).
Santa Fe County Probate Records, Wills and Testaments, Book A-1.
Santa Fe County Probate Records, Bonds of Administrators and Guardians of
    Estates, Book A-1, 1851–64.
Santa Fe County Probate Records, Probate Case File 1005 no. 87.
Santa Fe County Records, Deed Book B, C, D, L, N, Y.
Santa Fe County Records, District Court Record of 1847 Treason Trials,
    Warrant Book 1848–54.
Santa Fe County Records, Probate Court Journal, 1848–56.
Santa Fe County Treasurer, Warrant Book 1848–54.
Secretary of State Collection, Laws of New Mexico, 1852, 1878.
Spanish Archives of N.Mex. I.
    Juan B. Vigil List of Property Owners, 1836.
    Trinidad Barceló Letter to Government Secretary, 1846.
Spanish Archives of N.Mex. II.
    List of Friars involved in gambling, 1817.
    Surveyor General Report No. 21, Town of Tajique Grant.
Territorial Archives of N.Mex.
    Torrance County District Court Records, Civil Court Case No. 110.
    U.S. Census Records of N.Mex. for 1850–80, 1900.
    U.S. District Court Records, First Judicial District, Santa Fe County 1850,
        1851, 1852, and 1853.
    Valencia County Probate Journal A, Administracion de la estado de la
        difunto Maria de la Luz Barselo.
New York Historical Society.
    Major Henry Lane Kendrick to brother, Puebla, Mexico, Jan. 13, 1848,
        Misc. mss.
Newport Historical Society.
    Unidentified and undated newspaper clipping.
Puy-de-Dôme, Department of. Archives. Clermont-Ferrand, France.
    Lempdes Baptisms, 1814.

St. Louis Mercantile Library.
    Journal of Henry G. A. Caspers, 1846–47.
State of Virginia, Clarke County, Nomination Form 1969, National Register of
    Historic Places Inventory.
University of Arizona.
    Archivo de la Mitra de Sonora and Sinaloa.
    Guide to Parish Archives of Sonora and Sinaloa.
University of Missouri Western Historical Manuscript Collection–Columbia
    and State Historical
        John Sappington Collection 1027, Folder 45. Theodore D. Wheaton to
            Doct. Sappington, Savannah [Mo.], Mar. 6, 1844.
Society of Missouri Manuscripts Joint Collection.
University of North Carolina.
    Jeremy Francis Gilmer Papers, Lenoir Family Papers, No. 2, Nov. 6, 1846.
University of Virginia Library.
    Diary of Anna Maria Morris, Manuscript 3448.

Unpublished Sources
"City of Santa Fe, New Mexico, Memo," to Archaeological Review Committee
    from Mary G. Ragins, Case ARC-9-99. Typescript, Aug. 19, 1999.

Government Documents
U.S. House of Representatives. *Message from the President of the United States,
    Containing the Report of Secretary of War Conrad for 1851. Statement of
    Buildings Rented by the Quartermaster's Department at the Post of Santa
    Fe, New Mexico.* H. Doc., Ex. Doc. 2, 32nd Cong., 1st sess.
U.S. Senate. *Report of the Secretary of Interior upon Claims for Depredations by
    Indians in the Territory of New Mexico, May 12, 1858.* S. Doc., Ex. Doc. 55,
    35th Cong., 1st sess.

Interviews
Kate Torres Baca, Socorro, N.Mex., Feb. 11, 1989.
Tomás Barceló, Agustín Barceló, Moctezuma; Francisco Durazo Moreno,
    Huásabas; and Jorge Provencio Barceló, Granados, Sonora, Mexico, May
    4–5, 1986.
Martin J. Bode, Jr., Santa Fe, N.Mex., Feb. 4, 1989.
David Gallegos, Santa Fe, N.Mex., Dec. 10, 1984.
Ruben (Ruby) Gomez, Pagosa Springs, Colo., Sept. 10, 1986.
Bertha Wheaton Gatlin Mascareñas, Taos, N.Mex., Apr. 8, 1988.
Tony Mignardot, Santa Fe, N.Mex., Feb. 25, 1985.
Margaret Racel, Albuquerque, N.Mex., Jan. 14, 1985 and Jan. 10, 2006.
Petra Giddings Riddle, Santa Fe, N.Mex., Dec. 29, 1984.

Correspondence

Richard D. Bokum to M. J. Cook, Miami, Fl., Jan. 24, 1989.
Homer E. Milford to M. J. Cook, Santa Fe, N.Mex., Jan 23, 1997.
Gerd Alfred Petermann to M. J. Cook, Richmond Heights, Mo., June 26, 1991.

Newspapers

Albuquerque Journal
Daily New Mexican, and various names
Die Tägliche Deutsche Tribüne, St. Louis
Lubbock Avalanche-Journal, Tex.
Missouri Daily Republican
New Mexican Review
New Orleans Picayune
New York Times
New York Daily Tribune
Newport Mercury, R.I.
Niles' National Register
Revista Oficial, Chihuahua
Santa Fe Reporter
Santa Fe Weekly Gazette
St. Louis Republican
St. Louis Reveille
Stroud Messenger, Okla.

Printed Sources

Abert, J. W. *Report of Lieut. J. W. Abert of His Examination of New Mexico, in the Years 1846–1847*. 30th Cong., 1st sess., House Exec. Doc. No. 41 [Serial 517]. Washington, D.C.: Wendell and Van Benthuysen, 1848.

Allison, W. W. H. "Santa Fe in 1846, Recollections of Col. Francisco Perea." *Old Santa Fe* 2, no. 4 (Apr. 1915).

Anderson, George B., comp. *History of New Mexico*. New York: Pacific States Publishing, 1907.

Archivo de Simancas, Catalogo 12, Secretaria de Guerra. Valladolid, 1958.

"Arroyo Hondo, Penitentes, Weddings, Wakes." *El Palacio* 81, no. 1 (Mar. 1975).

Baca, Oswald G. "Analysis of Deaths in New Mexico's Río Abajo during the Late Spanish Colonial and Mexican Periods, 1793–1846." *New Mexico Historical Review* 70, no. 3 (July 1995).

———. "Infectious Diseases and Smallpox Politics in New Mexico's Rio Abajo, 1847–1920." *New Mexico Historical Review* 75, no. 1 (Jan. 2000).

Ballesteros, Selina, Ruth Benander, and Jeff Moline. "History of Settlement and Community: The Barrio del Torreon, Santa Fe, New Mexico." *Ethnohistory of the Southwest*, Colorado College, 1985.

Bancroft, Hubert Howe. *History of Arizona and New Mexico 1530–1888*. Vol. 17. San Francisco: The History Company, 1889.

Bandelier, Adolph F. *The Southwestern Journals of Adolph F. Bandelier 1883–1884*. Edited and annotated by Charles H. Lange and Carroll L. Riley. Albuquerque: University of New Mexico Press, 1970.

Barker, Ruth Laughlin. *Caballeros: The Romance of Santa Fe and the Southwest*. New York: D. Appleton, 1931.

Barreiro, Antonio. "Ojeada sobre Nuevo Mexico." Edited and translated by Lansing B. Bloom. 2 parts. *New Mexico Historical Review* 3 (Jan.–Apr. 1828).

Barry, Louise. *The Beginning of the West 1540–1854*. Topeka: Kansas State Historical Society, 1972.

Baxter, William. *The Gold of the Ortiz Mountains: A Story of New Mexico and the West's First Major Gold Rush. Santa Fe*. Santa Fe, N.Mex.: Lone Butte Press, 2004.

Bek, William G. "The Followers of Duden." In Gustavus Wulfing, "Twelfth Article." *Missouri Historical Review* 17, no. 1 (October 1922).

Bennassar, Bartolomé. *The Spanish Character: Attitudes and Mentalities from the Sixteenth to the Nineteenth Century*. Berkeley: University of California Press, 1979.

Bennett, James A. *Forts and Forays*. Edited by Clinton E. Brooks and Frank D. Reeve. Albuquerque: University of New Mexico Press, 1948.

Bieber, Ralph P., ed. *Journal of a Soldier under Kearny and Doniphan*. Glendale, Calif.: Arthur H. Clark, 1935.

———. *Southern Trails to California in 1849*. Vol. 5. Glendale, Calif.: Arthur H. Clark, 1937.

Bloom, Lansing, ed. "Minutes of the New Mexico Historical Society 1859–1863." *New Mexico Historical Review* 18, no. 3 (July 1943).

———. "New Mexico under Mexican Administration, 1822–1846." *Old Santa Fe* 1, no. 1 (July 1913) and no. 3 (Jan. 1914).

Bourke, John G. *An Apache Campaign in the Sierra Madre*. New York: Charles Scribner's Sons, 1958.

Boyle, Susan Calafate. *Commerciantes, Arrieros, y Peones: The Hispanos and the Santa Fe Trade*. Santa Fe: National Park Service, Southwest Region, 1994.

Brayer, Herbert Oliver. *William Blackmore: The Spanish-Mexican Land Grants of New Mexico and Colorado, 1863–1878*. 2 Vols. Denver: Bradford-Robinson, 1949.

Brewerton, G. Douglass. "Incidents of Travel in New Mexico." *Harper's New Monthly Magazine* 47 (Apr. 1854).

Burr, Anna Robeson Brown. *The Golden Quicksand*. New York: D. Appleton-Century, 1936.

Cabeza de Baca, Fabiola. "Don Gaspar Ortiz y Alari—Alcalde and Piñon King." *The Santa Fe Scene*, Sept. 13, 1958.

Calderón de la Barca, Fanny. *Life in Mexico: The Letters of Fanny Calderón*. Edited and annotated by Howard T. Fisher and Marion Hall Fisher. Garden City, N.Y.: Doubleday, Anchor Book edition, 1970.

Chacón, Rafael. *Legacy of Honor: The Life of Rafael Chacón, a Nineteenth-Century New Mexican*. Edited by Jacqueline Dorgan Meketa. Albuquerque: University of New Mexico Press, 1986.

Chaput, Donald. *François X. Aubry: Trader, Trailmaker, and Voyageur in the Southwest, 1846–1854*. Glendale, Calif.: Arthur H. Clark, 1975.

Chávez, Angélico. "Doña Tules, Her Fame and Her Funeral." *El Palacio* 57, no. 8 (Aug. 1950).

———. *New Mexico Roots: Diligencias Matrimoniales (Prenuptial Investigations)*. 12 vols. Vols. 10, 11, 12. Santa Fe: Privately published, 1982.

———. "Notes and Documents." *New Mexico Historical Review* 31, nos. 9–10 (Jan. 1856).

———. *Origins of New Mexico Families: A Genealogy of the Spanish Colonial Period*. Rev. ed. Santa Fe: Museum of New Mexico Press, 1992.

Chávez, Fray Angélico, and Thomas E. Chávez. *Wake for a Fat Vicar: Father Juan Felipe Ortiz, Archbishop Lamy, and the New Mexican Catholic Church in the Middle of the Nineteenth Century*. Albuquerque: LPD Press, 2004.

Chávez, Thomas E. *Manuel Alvarez, 1794–1856: A Southwestern Biography*. Niwot: University Press of Colorado, 1990.

Clark, Robert Emmet. *Community of Property and the Family in New Mexico*. Albuquerque: University of New Mexico Press, 1956.

Cleland, Robert Glass. *This Reckless Breed of Men: The Trappers and Fur Traders of the Southwest*. New York: Alfred A. Knopf, 1950.

Connelley, William Elsey. *Doniphan's Expedition*. Topeka, Kan.: Published by the author, 1907.

Cook, Mary Jean. "Gertrudis Barceló, Woman Entrepreneur of the Chihuahua and Santa Fe Trails, 1830–1850." In *El Camino Real de Tierra Adentro*, compiled by Gabrielle G. Palmer and Stephen L. Fosberg. Vol. 2. Santa Fe: Bureau of Land Management, New Mexico State Office, 1999.

———. "Governor James S. Calhoun Remembered." *Wagon Tracks, Santa Fe Trail Association Quarterly* 8, no. 2 (Feb. 1994).

———. *Loretto: The Sisters and Their Santa Fe Chapel*. Rev. ed. Santa Fe: Museum of New Mexico Press, 2002.

———. "Pizarro and Doña Tules at the Palace." *Compadres, Newsletter of the Palace of the Governors* 3 (1994).

———. "¿Porqué Monterey? The Death and Mysterious Burial of Merchant Manuel Alvarez, Part 1." *Wagon Tracks, Santa Fe Trail Association Quarterly* 19, no. 2 (May 2005).

Dabney, William M., and Josiah C. Russell, eds. *Historical Essays.* Albuquerque: University of New Mexico Press, 1952.

Davis, W. W. H. *El Gringo: New Mexico and Her People.* Reprint. Lincoln: University of Nebraska Press, 1982.

Dictionary of American Biography. Vols. 13, 19.

Dunham, Harold H. "Cerán St. Vrain." *Mountain Men and the Fur Trade.* 10 Vols. Edited by LeRoy R. Hafen. Glendale, Calif.: Arthur H. Clark, 1965–72.

Egan, Martha J. *Relicarios: Devotional Miniatures from the Americas.* Santa Fe: Museum of New Mexico Press, 1993.

Elliott, Richard Smith. *The Mexican War Correspondence of Richard Smith Elliott.* Edited and annotated by Mark L. Gardner and Marc Simmons. Norman: University of Oklahoma Press, 1997.

Ellis, Bruce. *Bishop Lamy's Santa Fe Cathedral.* Albuquerque: University of New Mexico Press, 1985.

———. "Fraud without Scandal: The Rogue Lovato Grant and Gaspar Ortiz y Alarid." *New Mexico Historical Review* 57, no. 1 (Jan. 1982).

Emmett, Chris. *Fort Union and the Winning of the West.* Norman: University of Oklahoma Press, 1965.

Enciclopedia Salvat, Diccionario. Tomo 2. Barcelona, Spain: Salvat Editiones, S.A., n.d.

Espinosa, Gilberto, and Tibo J. Chavez. *El Río Abajo.* Portales, N.Mex.: Bishop Publishing, n.d.

Espinosa, J. Manuel. "Memoir of a Kentuckian in New Mexico 1848–1884." *New Mexico Historical Review* 13, no. 1 (Jan. 1937).

Ferguson, Erna. *New Mexico.* New York: Alfred A. Knopf, 1950.

The Gamblers. Alexandria, Va.: Time-Life Books, 1978.

Garrard, Lewis H. *Wah-to-yah and The Taos Trail.* Norman: University of Oklahoma Press, 1955, 1972.

Gibson, George Rutledge. *A Soldier under Kearny and Doniphan, 1846–1847.* Edited by Ralph P. Bieber. Glendale, Calif.: Arthur H. Clark, 1935.

Glasgow, Edward James, and William Henry Glasgow. *Brothers on the Santa Fe and Chihuahua Trails: Edward James Glasgow and William Henry Glasgow, 1846–1848.* Edited and annotated by Mark L. Gardner. Niwot: University Press of Colorado, 1993.

González, Deena J. *Refusing the Favor: The Spanish-Mexican Women of Santa Fe 1820–1880.* New York: Oxford University Press, 1999.

Grant, Blanche C. *Doña Lona: A Story of Taos and Santa Fe.* New York: Wilfred Funk, 1941.

Gregg, Josiah. *Commerce of the Prairies.* Edited by Max L. Moorhead. Norman: University of Oklahoma Press, 1954.

Hafen, LeRoy R., ed. *Ruxton of the Rockies.* Norman: University of Oklahoma Press, 1979.

Hall, Thomas B. *Medicine on the Santa Fe Trail*. Dayton, Ohio: Morningside Book Shop, 1971.

Hanks, Nancy. *Lamy's Legion: The Individual Histories of Secular Clergy Serving in the Archdiocese of Santa Fe from 1850 to 1912*. Santa Fe: HRM Books, 2000.

Harlow, Neal. *California Conquered: War and Peace on the Pacific, 1846–1850*. Berkeley: University of California Press, 1982.

Heitman, Francis B. *Historical Register and Dictionary of the U.S. Army, 1789–1903*. Washington, D.C.: Government Printing Office, 1903.

Hinchey, William James. "William James Hinchey: An Irish Artist on the Santa Fe Trail." *Wagon Tracks, Santa Fe Trail Association Quarterly*. Edited by Anna Belle Cartwright. Part I, 10, no. 3 (May 1996); Part II, 10, no. 4 (Aug. 1996); Part III, 11, no. 1 (Nov. 1996).

History of Andrew and De Kalb Counties, Missouri. St. Louis: Goodspeed Publishing, 1888.

History of Buchanan County, Missouri. St. Joseph, Mo.: Union Historical, 1881.

History of Saline County, Missouri. St. Louis: Missouri Historical, 1881.

Horgan, Paul. *Lamy of Santa Fe, His Life and Times*. New York: Farrar, Straus and Giroux, 1975.

Huning, Franz. *Trader on the Santa Fe Trail: Memoirs of Franz Huning*. Albuquerque: University of New Mexico Press, 1973.

Hunt, Aurora. *Kirby Benedict: Frontier Federal Judge (1853–1874)*. Glendale, Calif.: Arthur H. Clark, 1961.

James, Thomas. *Three Years among the Indians and Mexicans*. Edited by Walter B. Douglas. St. Louis: Missouri Historical Society, 1916.

Jaramillo, Cleofas M. *Shadows of the Past*. Santa Fe: Seton Village Press, 1941.

Jenkins, Myra Ellen. "The Donaciano Vigil House." *Bulletin of the Historic Santa Fe Foundation* 12, no. 3 (Dec. 1984).

Kaye, E. Donald. "Specie on the Santa Fe Trail." *Wagon Tracks, Santa Fe Trail Association Quarterly* 14, no. 4 (Aug. 2000).

Kennerly, William Clark. *Persimmon Hill: A Narrative of Old St. Louis and the Far West*. Norman: University of Oklahoma Press, 1948.

Kingsbury, John M. *Trading in Santa Fe: John M. Kingsbury's Correspondence with James Josiah Webb, 1853–1861*. Edited by Jane Lenz Elder and David J. Weber. Dallas, Tex.: Southern Methodist University Press, 1996.

Kubler, George. *The Religious Architecture of New Mexico in the Colonial Period and Since the American Occupation*. Colorado Springs: Taylor Museum, 1940.

Lane, Lydia Spencer. *I Married a Soldier*. Albuquerque, N.Mex.: Horn and Wallace, 1964.

Larpenteur, Charles. *Forty Years a Fur Trader on the Upper Missouri*. Edited with notes by Elliott Coues. 2 Vols. New York: Francis P. Harper, 1898.

Laughlin (Alexander), Ruth. *The Wind Leaves No Shadow.* Caldwell, Idaho: Caxton Printers, 1948.

Lecompte, Janet. "The Independent Women of Hispanic New Mexico, 1821–1846." *Western Historical Quarterly* 12 (Jan. 1981).

———. "Manuel Armijo and the Americans." In *Spanish and Mexican Land Grants in New Mexico and Colorado,* edited by John R. And Christine M. Van Ness. Boulder, Colorado: Colorado Humanities Program, 1980; this also appears as an article in *Journal of the West* (July 1980) with additional material added.

———. *Rebellion in Río Arriba.* Albuquerque: University of New Mexico Press, 1985.

Leyva, Francis Paco. "Vignette of Huasabas, Sonora." *Cochise Quarterly* 20, no. 4 (winter 1991).

Lummis, Charles F. *Mesa, Cañon, and Pueblo.* New York: Century, 1925.

Magoffin, Susan. *Down the Santa Fe Trail and into Mexico: The Diary of Susan Shelby Magoffin 1846–1847.* Edited by Stella M. Drumm. Santa Fe: William Gannon, 1975.

Mattison, Ray H. "David Dawson Mitchell." In *The Mountain Men and the Fur Trade of the Far West,* edited by LeRoy R. Hafen. 10 Vols. Glendale, Calif.: Arthur H. Clark, 1965–72.

McCall, George Archibald. *New Mexico in 1850: A Military View.* Edited by Robert W. Frazer. Norman: University of Oklahoma, 1968.

McGaw, William Cochran. *Savage Scene: The Life and Times of James Kirker, Frontier King.* New York: Hastings House, 1972.

Meketa, Jacqueline, ed. *Legacy of Honor: The Life of Rafael Chacón, a Nineteenth-Century New Mexican.* Albuquerque: University of New Mexico Press, 1986.

———. *From Martyrs to Murderers: The Old Southwest's Saints, Sinners, and Scalawags.* Las Cruces, N.Mex.: Yucca Tree Press, 1993.

Meyer, Marian. *Mary Donoho: New First Lady of the Santa Fe Trail.* Santa Fe: Ancient City Press, 1991.

Mission Dolores Brochure, n.d.

Moorhead, Max L. *New Mexico's Royal Road: Trade and Travel on the Chihuahua Trail.* Norman: University of Oklahoma Press, 1958.

Morley, Sylvanus Griswold. "Santa Fe Architecture." *Old Santa Fe Magazine* 2 (1915).

Murphy, Lawrence R. "The Beaubien and Miranda Land Grant, 1841–1846." *New Mexico Historical Review* 42 (Jan. 1967).

Nentvig, Juan S. J. *Rudo Ensayo: A Description of Sonora and Arizona in 1764.* Translated, clarified, and annotated by Alberto Francisco Pradeau and Robert R. Rasmussen. Tucson: University of Arizona Press, 1980.

Northrop, Marie E. *Spanish-Mexican Families of Early California: 1769–1850.* Vol. 1. New Orleans: Polyanthos, 1976.

"Notes and Documents." *New Mexico Historical Review* 22, no. 4 (Oct. 1947).

Old Santa Fe. Vols. 1 (1913) and 2 (1915).

Oliva, Leo E. *Fort Union and the Frontier Army in the Southwest.* Santa Fe: Division of History, National Park Service, 1993.

Parrish, William J. "The German Jew." *New Mexico Historical Review* 35 (Jan. 1960).

Pérez, Demetrio. "Rasgo Histórico." In "New Notes on Bishop Lamy's First Years in New Mexico," edited by Bruce T. Ellis. *El Palacio* 65 (Feb. 1958).

Pfefferkorn, Ignaz. *Sonora: A Description of the Province.* Albuquerque: University of New Mexico Press, 1949.

Pike, Zebulon Montgomery. *The Journals of Zebulon Montgomery Pike.* Edited and annotated by Donald Jackson. 2 Vols. Norman: University of Oklahoma, 1966.

Prince, L. Bradford, compiler. *The General Laws of New Mexico; Including All the Unrepealed General Laws from the Promulgation of the "Kearney Code" in 1846, to the End of the Legislative Session of 1880.* Albany, N.Y.: W. C. Little, Law Publishers, 1882.

———. *Historical Sketches of New Mexico.* New York: Leggatt Brothers, 1893.

Read, Benjamin. *Illustrated History of New Mexico.* Santa Fe: New Mexican Printing, 1912.

Richardson, Albert D. *Beyond the Mississippi.* Philadelphia: American Publishing, 1867.

Rickey, Don, Jr. *Forty Miles on Beans and Hay: The Enlisted Soldier Fighting the Indian Wars.* Norman: University of Oklahoma Press, 1963.

Risch, Erna. *Quartermaster Support of the Army: A History of the Corps, 1775–1939.* Washington, D.C.: Center of Military History, United States Army, 1989.

Robeson, Anna Brown [Burr]. *The Gold Quicksand.* New York: D. Appleton-Century, 1936.

Rubio, Dario. *Refranes, Proverbios y Dichos y Dicharachos Mexicanos.* Tome I. 2nd ed. Méjico, D.F.: Editorial A.P. Márquez, 1940.

Ruxton, George Frederick. *Ruxton of the Rockies.* Collected by Clyde and Mae Reed Porter, edited by LeRoy R. Hafen. Norman: University of Oklahoma Press, 1950.

Sabin, Edwin L. *The Rose of Santa Fe.* New York: A. L. Burt, 1923.

Salcido, Francisco Jaime L., compiler. *Marcas y Señales para Ganado.* Estado de Sonora, 1963.

Sánchez, Joseph P. *Spanish Bluecoats: The Catalonian Volunteers in Northwestern New Spain, 1767–1810.* Albuquerque: University of New Mexico Press, 1990.

Santa Fe City Directory, 1930–31, 1936–37, 1950. El Paso, Tex.: Hudspeth Directory.

Sena, Col. José D. "The Chapel of Don Antonio José Ortiz." *New Mexico Historical Review* 13, no. 4 (October 1938).

Seton [Chase], Anya. *The Turquoise*. Chicago: Peoples Book Club, 1946; originally published by Houghton Mifflin, Boston.

Sherman, John. *Santa Fe: A Pictorial History*. Rev. 2d ed. Virginia Beach, Calif.: Donning, 1996.

Simmons, Marc. *Kit Carson and His Three Wives*. Albuquerque: University of New Mexico Press, 2003.

———. *Little Lion of the Southwest: A Life of Manuel Antonio Chaves*. Chicago: Swallow Press, 1973.

———. *Murder on the Santa Fe Trail: An International Incident, 1843*. El Paso, Tex.: Texas Western Press, 1987.

———. "New Mexico's Money Crunch." *Santa Fe Republican*, April 15–21, 1998.

———. "A Problem with Mule Packing Terminology." *Wagon Tracks, Santa Fe Trail Association Quarterly* 10 (May 1996).

———. *Spanish Government in New Mexico*. Albuquerque: University of New Mexico Press, 1986.

Simpson, James H. *Navaho Expedition: Journal of a Military Reconnaissance from Santa Fe, New Mexico, to the Navaho Country made in 1849 by Lieutenant James H. Simpson*. Edited and annotated by Frank McNitt. Norman: University of Oklahoma Press, 1964.

Sisneros, Francisco. "Paternal Line Genealogy of Francisco Sisneros." *Herencia* (Quarterly Journal of the Hispanic Genealogical Research Center of New Mexico) 3 (Apr. 1995).

Sisneros, Francisco, and Joe H. Torres. *Nombres*. Bernalillo, N.Mex.: Las Campanas Publications, 1982.

Stewart, Jay. *¡Viva Santa Fe!* Musical, 1991.

Stratton, Porter A. *The Territorial Press of New Mexico, 1834–1912* Albuquerque: University of New Mexico Press, 1969.

Sunder, John E., ed. *Matt Field on the Santa Fe Trail*. Norman: University of Oklahoma Press, 1966.

Thomas, Alfred B., ed. "An Anonymous Description of New Mexico, 1818." *Southwestern Historical Quarterly* 33, no. 11 (July 1929).

———. *Teodoro de Croix and the Northern Frontier of New Spain, 1776–1783*. Norman: University of Oklahoma Press, 1941.

Thrapp, Dan L. *Encyclopedia of Frontier Biography*. Glendale, Calif.: Arthur H. Clark, 1988.

Torrez, Robert J. "Governor Allende's Instructions for Conducting Caravans on the Camino Real, 1816." In *El Camino Real de Tierra Adentro*, compiled by Gabrielle G. Palmer and Stephen L. Fosberg, edited by June-el Piper. Santa Fe: Bureau of Land Management, New Mexico State Office, 1999.

Towne, Jackson S. "Printing in New Mexico." *New Mexico Historical Review* 35 (1960).

Townley, John M. "El Placer: A New Mexico Mining Boom Before 1846." *Journal of the West* 10, no. 1 (Jan. 1971).

Twitchell, Ralph Emerson. *The Leading Facts of New Mexico.* 5 Vols. 1883; Albuquerque: Horn and Wallace, 1963.

———. *Old Santa Fe.* 1925; Chicago: Rio Grande Press, 1963.

Tyler, Dan. "Governor Armijo's Moment of Truth." In *The Mexican War: Changing Interpretations,* edited by Odie B. Faulk and Joseph A. Stout Jr. Chicago: Swallow Press, 1973.

U.S. Census for New Mexico. Censuses for 1850, 1860, 1870, and 1880.

Verdon, Paul E. "David Dawson Mitchell: Virginian on the Wild Missouri." *Magazine of Montana* 27, no. 2 (spring 1977).

Vigil, Julián José. "Mis Tiempos." *La Herencia* 36 (winter 2002).

Voss, Stuart F. *On the Periphery of Nineteenth-Century Mexico: Sonora and Sinaloa, 1810–1877.* Tucson: The University of Arizona Press, 1982.

Waugh, Alfred S. *Travels in Search of the Elephant: The Wanderings of Alfred S. Waugh, Artist, in Louisiana, Missouri, and Santa Fe, in 1845–1846.* Edited by John Francis McDermott. St. Louis: Missouri Historical Society, 1951.

Weigle, Marta. *Brothers of Light, Brothers of Blood.* Albuquerque: University of New Mexico Press, 1976.

West, Robert C. *Sonora: Its Geographical Personality.* Austin: University of Texas Press, 1993.

Willard, Doctor. "Tour, or Inland Trade with New Mexico." In *Early Western Travels, 1748–1846,* edited by Reuben Gold Thwaites. Vol. 18. Cleveland: Arthur H. Clark, 1904–7.

Witham, Lydia Frances. *Garden of the World.* Edited by H. S. Foote. Chicago: Lewis Publishing, 1888.

Withers, Mrs. Robert S., ed. "Letters of a College Boy." *Missouri Historical Society Bulletin* 6, no. 1 (Oct. 1949).

Woodruff, M. Howard W. "Doniphan's Expedition—War with Mexico, 1846." *Missouri Miscellany* 11 (Mar. 1981).

Wroth, William. *Images of Penance, Images of Mercy: Southwestern Santos in the Late Nineteenth Century.* Norman: University of Oklahoma Press, 1991.

Young, Otis. *The West of Philip St. George Cooke, 1809–1895.* Glendale, Calif.: Arthur H. Clark, 1955.

Index

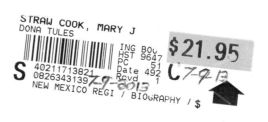